AN INTRODUCTION TO CHRISTIAN FAITH

AN
INTRODUCTION
TO
CHRISTIAN
FAITH

Walter Kasper

Paulist Press • New York • Ramsey

First published in this translation in 1980 by Burns & Oates, 2/10
Jerdan Place, London SW6 5PT in Britain and associated territories
and in Ireland; and by the **Paulist Press**, 545 Island Road, Ramsey,
N.J. 07446 in the United States of America.

First published in German in 1972 and in a fourth edition in 1975 by
Matthias-Grunewald-Verlag, Mainz, Federal Republic of Germany;
copyright © 1972, 1975 Matthias-Grunewald-Verlag, Mainz.
This translation by V. Green
copyright © 1980 Search Press, Ltd.

Library of Congress
Catalog Card Number: 80-82808

ISBN: 0-8091-2324-X (USA)
ISBN: 0 86012 080 5 (UK)

Printed and bound in the
United States of America

Contents

Dedicated to Heinrich Fries on his sixtieth birthday

Preface

The ten chapters of this book are the result of an experiment carried out a few years ago in the Faculty of Catholic Theology at Münster and in the Faculty of Catholic Theology at Tübingen. The initial stimulus was a frequently expressed wish for some kind of orientation among the various persuasions of contemporary theology, and for a more effective union of theory and practice. To answer this need, the lectures on which this introduction is based were delivered as a series for priests, teachers of religion and catechetics. They also served as an introductory course for students of systematic theology. The series of lectures I gave to this somewhat mixed audience was one of my most pleasant academic experiences to date.

To be sure, some readers will ask whether these lectures are progressive or conservative, and whether they are intended to be critical of society and Church or to buttress the existing system. Such notions do not really concern me. I tried to talk about theology as such and my impression was that my audience required and received just this. The rethinking with which the Church and theologians are concerned at present can succeed only if it is directed to the centre and takes effect from it. Faith has to do with that midpoint, for it comprises the unity and whole of Christian and church life. Therefore it is necessary to resist the demands of the modern age when we reach this central and fundamental point. That is the only way in which theology can really help the Church to adapt itself to the present-day world.

Of course the following pages show clearly that theology has to do with church reform and social respon-

sibility. But I hope that this book will also
demonstrate that theology does not have to go to in-
appropriate, even nonsensical, lengths in order to
prove itself vital and interesting. If theology attends
to its proper concerns and puts the emphasis on a
living understanding of faith (*fides quaerens intellec-
tum*), then it will automatically testify against the
lack of hope and faith characteristic of reactionaries
within the Church. I refer to those who take disciplin-
ary measures and play every possible trick only because they do not really trust in their essential
concern, and are not convinced that today it can have
any real chance of success. If theology looks to its real
interests then it is also an assertion of faith and hope
against that idiotic flight ahead in which a rich heri-
tage is squandered for a dish of pottage – the questionable applause of those who anyway are already
sure that faith is meaningless. Conservatives and progressives are very much alike in this regard.

With such warnings to right and left I am content
to take up a position between the claims of existing
parties. The slogans and catch-calls which evoke the
approval of one side or the other are easily learnt.
Theological reflection, however, is more responsible
than that. Reflection means making distinctions. In a
situation in which discrimination is disavowed as dis-
honourable and weak, it is salutary to recall the profound skills of scholastic disputation with its *pro et
contra*. The centre is not a harmless geometrical point
but a field of tension that endures in spite of all that
is extreme and in fact can be described only in relation
to the extreme. For this reason it is easier to maintain
extreme positions, whereas mediation demands spiritual strength. We need an increase of the strength to
fight 'between the front-lines'. In contradistinction to
the widespread triumphalist myth that modern the-

ology has diverged considerably from tradition, I find
the present state of theology very dismal. Where
among the confusing multitude of theological papers,
articles and books do we find a convincing new approach or any truly impressive project that can be
compared in even the remotest way with the great
works of tradition?

This book does not claim to be anything like a new
mini-summa of theology. Nevertheless it is offered as
an introduction to essential questions of systematic
theology, and as a specific systematic approach to
them. It is not designed to impress but as a spur to
thought. My intention is to show that Christian faith
can be presented responsibly even in the face of modern thought, and that modern theology, if it is pursued
seriously, does not produce confusion but promotes the
express concern of this book's last chapter: that dimension of faith which we call hope.

I should like above all to thank my audiences in
Münster and Tübingen. Their questions and remarks
have been included in this final version. I also thank
my research assistants, Dr G. Greshake and H. Tief-
enbacher, as well as B. Schrott and Frau A. Buck, for
help in producing the book. I dedicate it to one of my
teachers who at a very early date introduced me to the
rich variety of a theology of the creative centre: Heinrich Fries.

Walter Kasper

1 The situation of faith

1.1 Crisis or turning-point of faith

It was Goethe who said that all history was a struggle between belief and unbelief. Many people think that that contest is over. They would say that now it is pointless, or that it has already been decided in favour of the opponents of belief. As far as they are concerned, the contest between belief and unbelief is now no more than a quibble about words on the validity of which it is impossible to say anything certain. Therefore they find the debate on faith meaningless. If that is so, then Hegel's and Nietzsche's notion of the death of God[1] seems a more appropriate description of our present social and spiritual situation.

Of course the highly-ambiguous concept of the death of God is not intended as an assertion that God has died in the ordinary sense of exit from mortal, historical existence. Any such statement would be obviously nonsensical. Nor does it mean that God 'is' not, for strictly speaking the assertion of the non-existence of God is as impossible to demonstrate as the contrary proposition that he exists. Talk of the death of God means much more that God is dead in the sense that belief in him affords no impulse of any kind that might be said to determine human life and human history; that he is no longer a living presence in our lives; and that the pronouncements of believers are no longer appropriate to real human problems and experience. They no longer correspond to any problem or question and therefore people cannot treat them as anything other than uplift or provocation – a mild stimulus. The gulf between faith and human experience is therefore one of the most intractable problems of contemporary preaching and theology. Because of this gap many people treat not only God but the God-question itself as dead. A concerned atheist whose heart is uneasy until it finds refuge in God (Augustine) is already almost a 'pastoral windfall' (Karl Rahner).

This widespread indifference to religion has resulted (at least in the western world) in a relaxation of external pressure on the Church. That in its turn has produced a degree of freedom and discussion within the Church that was impossible in the last few centuries, which for the Church were characterized much more by defensiveness and integrism. Only today are we able to engage in open confrontation and positive encounter with the modern age. That however has led to a second phenomenon of a state of crisis: to a pluralism of opinions and to a polarization of viewpoints.[2]

To be sure there were in the past differing theological schools and various forms of piety and devotion. But the differences existed more or less within a common environment and a horizon of understanding that everyone acknowledged. It was possible to make out another person's or party's position accurately, and to say exactly where and why one disagreed with it. Nowadays approaches to thought, conceptual categories, and the entire background of life and understanding have become so diverse that it is no longer possible to know and understand all the different positions, unless one were at some much higher level, from which vantage-point one could integrate and harmonize

them all proficiently. These differences do not only
affect peripheral questions and matters of formulation.
There are also increasingly varied and contradictory
ideas of what constitutes the very centre of the Christian message and the actual 'nature' or 'essence' of
Christianity. Hence the one faith of the Church is in
danger of losing its directness, unambiguousness and
power of witness.

Very many Christians experience all this as a crisis
of belief. Perplexed and even aghast, they observe the
infection of the Church too by the secular spirit. They
note that in the Church too, under the guise of pluralism and a new interpretation of Christian faith, the
barriers between truth and untruth have been dis-
mantled. They believe that in an age in which God's
immediate presence has been obscured the Church too
is experiencing a profound confusion of spirits and,
indeed, a decadence that reaches right down to its
basic principles. They point to various attempts to
reinterpret faith in an immanentist sense and to man-
ipulate it in conformity with mere ideologies that
peddle the message of salvation within this world.

No one with any insight at all would deny that there
are grounds for this kind of concern. But the common
features of such analyses are a plaintive, resigned tone
and a lack of trust in faith. It is part of the Church's
essential nature to be a battlefield of truth and lies.
The Church, which triumphs over all untruth, is an
eschatological beacon of hope.

As such it is a basis for courage and trust, and not
for complaints and accusations. The superficially deep
concern and assertion of belief that I have described
conceals not strong but weak faith. And anyone who
interprets *all* problems of the Church as *no more than*
a faith-crisis is treating things far too superficially.
Such critics presuppose that other positions are unjus-

tifiable from the start, and thereby withdraw from discussion, shunning the responsibility of changing anything at all in the Church, however small it may be. Such an attitude itself can be a lack of readiness for conversion, which is an essential part of faith.

Therefore we must be very careful when talking about a 'crisis of faith'. To the average person the word 'crisis' has a wholly negative ring about it. To most people talk of a crisis of faith is tantamount to talk of the collapse of faith. Yet 'crisis' in its original sense means a situation in which a decision has to be taken, or a decisive state of affairs. A critical situation is one in which the existing structures and forms are no longer obviously acceptable. This state of things offers a degree of free choice and opportunity for action. The future is open. Hence a crisis can lead to ruination but it can also be a fortunate turning-point. A crisis of faith can lead to a renewed and deeper understanding of faith. Such critical turning-points have constantly recurred in the history of the Church and of theology: three major instances are the Constantinian era, the Gregorian reform and the Reformation. In each case the faith had to preserve its identity throughout a vast process of historical change. It is possible that today we have arrived at a similar epoch-making time of change in the history of the Church and of dogma. The end-result is not predetermined; instead, and much more, it is something that we ourselves shall be called upon to decide. That is our situation at present, at this critical turning-point of history.

Therefore we have to ask: What does Christian faith mean in view of the modern state of things? How is it articulated and realized today? What place and task does it have in contemporary society? To obtain a clear view of the future in this regard we must first try to understand more precisely the present situation of belief. And that is possible only with the help of historical analysis; that alone will enable us to distinguish transient phenomena from lasting historical perspectives, and to reach clarity among the confusion of slogans. Hence we must view our situation in the larger context of spiritual, social and theological history.

1.2 The foundations of the modern age

If we are to understand our present age, we have to begin with the modern Enlightenment.[3] It is certainly the most significant revolution that has occurred in the West. The Enlightenment is far from done with today. On the contrary, only now are we experiencing its full effect. The Enlightenment is a process running through the entire cultural history of the western world. It began as early as the Ionian philosophers of nature, and recurred with the Sophists and Stoics, who even then tried to interpret myths rationally and to explain them allegorically. Hence we can agree with Hegel when he says that all western history is a process by which man gradually takes possession of his own freedom. At the beginning of the modern epoch, however, this history of freedom entered a new phase. Freedom and thought became self-aware and self-critical. Kant defined Enlightenment as 'man's emergence from the immaturity for which he himself is responsible. Immaturity is the inability to use one's understanding without the help of another . . . *Sapere aude!* Have the courage to make use of your own understanding! is therefore the motto of the Enlightenment'.[4]

Hence enlightenment is a process of emancipation. Man liberates himself from pre-established authority and tradition. He wants to see, judge and decide for himself. Nevertheless, though he comes into possession of himself in this way, his freedom is not arbitrary. Its standard and its criterion are to be found in itself. Man becomes the measure of man. Man becomes the reference-point of reality. He no longer sees himself as one element – however prominent – within a cosmos which is predetermined for him and which encompasses him; instead the world is much more to be conceived and projected from a human viewpoint and towards a human goal. It is in this sense that we speak of the 'anthropological turning-point', or of 'modern subjectivity'.

The modern focus on the human subject resulted in practice in a fundamental alteration of our entire socio-cultural world. On the political level it led to the recognition of the freedom and equality of all men, to the declaration of the universal rights of man, and thence to the French Revolution. It brought about the dissolution of the existing hierarchical and patriarchal social order and its replacement with a communal order of free and equal men, and thereby gave rise to a profound crisis of authority. Everyone who nowadays proclaims the basic democratic rights of freedom professes as he does so the fundamental concern of the Enlightenment. In the area of human knowledge the critical attitude of the modern period and the rejection of tradition made possible the modern experiential sciences. They have basically altered our picture of the world, and have led to a rational way of behaving and of using the world.

In a scientifically-ordered world it is not what tradition sanctifies but what is backed by rational discussion that carries the day. Science and technology enable man to make himself increasingly lord and master of the real world, to plan, control and mould it rationally. The result is a hominized and secularized world,[5] in which we encounter less and less often the

traces of God and more and more often the marks of
man. All that secularization means is man's self-lib-
eration from religious and metaphysically shaped be-
haviour-patterns and categories of thought, and the
way in which he gets used to orientating himself to
the immanent autonomy of the various areas of
reality.

The results for faith of this modern evolution are
evident in that Christianity has largely lost its position in the new world. The Christian picture of the
world and of humanity and its understanding of authority were profoundly affected and shaped by an
epoch that has now finally disappeared. The necessary result has been that Christian faith has been seen
as basically no more than the ideology of a past order
and a barrier to progress. To a certain extent, therefore, it is understandable that for a long time the
Church almost entirely looked on modern emancipation as an unfortunate departure from a theonomic
order, and condemned it as decadent and destructive.

There is hardly one major modern scientific discovery that has not been condemned or put under suspicion by at least one of the Churches. The case of
Galileo is merely the most famous instance of a wholly
inglorious series of condemnations. In this regard the
second Vatican Council was a turning-point. The
Council acknowledged the autonomy of the various
branches of secular culture and recognized the principle of religious freedom.[6] In so doing it took up decisive Enlightenment themes and accepted them as
legitimate in a Christian sense. That was the proper
course, for it was the Bible which for the first time
unequivocally expressed the inalienable dignity and
freedom of *all* men, their equality before God, and
therefore the brotherhood of all men. Even the two
creation stories in Genesis carry out what might be

called a 'denuminization' of the world, and make man
the lord of reality commissioned to subdue the world
to himself. Hence it is no accident that the modern
secularization process should have occurred on the
ground of a European civilization deeply moulded by
Christianity. Secularization is *also* an historico-cul-
tural and socio-historical product of Christianity,[7]
among other influences.

A revision of the Church's attitude to the modern
age is naturally something quite other than an und-
istanced and uncritical acceptance of all the theses of
the Enlightenment. In view of the French Revolution
and the Terror, Hegel already perceived the dangers
of a freedom posited as absolute and spoke of the 'fury
of dissolution'. In our own century we have been made
much more effectively aware of the 'dialectic of the
Enlightenment' (Max Horkheimer and Friedrich
Adorno): Surely a form of reflection which believes
that it can grasp reality must ultimately seize and
control man too . . . Surely a wholly critical form of
reason must ultimately efface itself . . . If thought
wants to stay truly critical and not self-righteous and
pharisaical then it must criticize itself. But surely that
takes the ground from under it . . .

It was Nietzsche above all who was courageous
enough to look at the full consequences of the modern
age. In the same context in which Nietzsche's madman
proclaims the death of God, he asks: 'What did we do
when we unchained this earth from its sun? Whither
is it now moving? Whither are we moving? Away from
all suns? Are we not ever rushing onwards? And back-
wards, sidewards, forwards, to all sides? Is there still
an above and a below? Are we not wandering in a
never-ending nothingness? Do we not feel the breath
of empty space? Has it not become colder? Is not night
and evermore night upon us?'[8] Does this mean that

nihilism is the ultimate consequence of emancipated thought?

Understandably the Church of the modern era and many modern thinkers drew back aghast from these consequences. Their fear gave rise to a second important current of modern thought: the philosophy of the 'Restoration.'[9] It has effectively determined the theology and practice of the Church, above all since the start of the nineteenth century. People like de Maistre, de Bonald, Cortes, Haller and so on recognized that human reason was essentially concerned with language, tradition and authority. According to them only authority could guarantee truth and order. In their view human freedom, since it is only possible historically and socially, can never be absolutely autonomous. Our understanding is orientated to language, tradition and community. Therefore belief (in the broad sense) precedes reason. A whole philosophy of authority arose in this way. Within theology this movement was initially expressed in the form of what is known as traditionalism, which was later condemned by the Church. More to the point, however, these ideas were a definitive influence on the movement which at the first Vatican Council led to the definition of papal primacy and infallibility. The council Fathers thought that they were helping a decadent world by giving it an orientation-point and a focus of unity in the papacy. The Church represented itself as the great supportive and maintaining power. As such it proved extremely attractive to many leading minds. This is shown above all by the great converts of the nineteenth and twentieth centuries: Brentano, Stolbert, Newman, Claudel, Wust and Maritain – to offer only a few names. They had all peered into the depths of the modern age and in their revulsion from it rediscovered support and a home in the Catholic Church.

In a certain sense we may see the second Vatican Council as a rejection of this 'restoration' mentality which was so opposed to the modern age. Of course such an opening up and out is impossible without crises.

At first sight the Church at Vatican II would appear to have surrendered what until then was its strength and made it attractive to so many great minds but also a refuge for all those looking for security. A really powerful revival of old-guard ideas is at the moment quite inconceivable. Restoration can never be a solution. Once authority is questioned, it can only be defended by itself taking to argument. And every argument evokes new questions. Any standpoint of authority has been deprived of strength by the spirit of Enlightenment. A restoration pure and simple is no longer possible. All that is still feasible for us is a critical relation to authority – which does not mean a negative relation. Nowadays authority has to show that it is a condition for and an enablement of freedom. That means that today we have to try to mediate in a positive and creative way between faith and modern thought, between the Church and modern society.

Such an attempt at mediation is not a new thing. It was the basic concern of the classical era of German intellectual history from Leibniz to Hegel – the so-called *Goethezeit*, or period of Goethe. Here we are concerned with the third great movement of the modern age. The attempt to mediate was made in high theological style by the Catholic Tübingen School of the nineteenth century: by J. S. Drey, J. B. Hirscher, J. A. Möhler, J. E. Kuhn and F. A. Staudenmaier.[10] Their theology is happily free of purely negative polemics and nervous apologetics. It tries to find a way to the opponent's real strength and thus to learn from him. Long before the words *aggiornamento* and dia-

logue almost became slogans, these Tübingen theologians were practising what the words really mean.
Many present difficulties would have been spared us
if they had not been displaced in the second half of the
last century by a short-sighted and short-lived restoration of neo-Scholasticism.

Problems can only be removed by solving them. The
problems unsolved at that time recurred in liberal
theology and in Modernism at the turn of the century.
In a much more direct and summary form they have
now reappeared in some forms of the 'theology of secularization', 'theology after the death of God', and the
'theology of revolution'. In each of these cases social
and cultural processes are forced to coincide with the
Christian message. All that happens is that the restrictions of neo-Scholasticism shift to new areas; they
have not been removed altogether. In neo-Scholasticism the critical and liberating force of the Gospel was
hidden under a form of Thomist philosophy adulter-
ated by Descartes and Wolff. In our own time something very similar is done by taking over certain
findings of the modern social and human sciences for
the most part in an amateurish way.

Lessing accurately perceived the dangers of *this*
kind of conciliatory theology. He talked of the 'liquid
manure' of fashionable theology, and rejected it on the
ground that all it did on the pretence of making us
into rational Christians was to turn us into highly
irrational philosophers.[11] That is to say: such a form
of mediation bears with it the danger that thought
and faith will be destroyed simultaneously. If both are
brought into harmony and neutralized, both lose their
bite and precision. Then the critical nature of modern
thought is repudiated, as is the critical and scandalizing nature of faith. As a result faith serves to justify
and propitiate the *status quo*; it becomes ideology. It

was Marx who put this charge of ideology in its classical and wholly memorable form: 'Religion is the general theory of this world, its encylopaedic compendium, its logic in popular form, its spiritual *point d'honneur*, its enthusiasm, its moral sanction, its solemn complement, its general basis of consolation and justification'.[12] This suspicion of ideology does not arise only when the Church and theology serve to justify conservative forces, but when they represent themselves as the vanguard of revolutionary movements and repeat in other terms what others have usually already said more effectively without their aid. Then the salt of Christian faith loses its savour just as much as before.

Kierkegaard above all offered a highly-nuanced description of the qualitative difference between Church and society. Karl Barth and the dialectical theologians of this century have produced an effective version of his criticism of idealistic attempts at mediation. God is acknowledged as the quite Other whom man can confront only in listening and obedience. Here the word of God is again critically maintained as against the false claims to autonomy made by human reason *and* a ghetto Church.

The emotive power of dialectical theology and its moderate Catholic advocates cannot of course gloss over the fact that they have done more to obscure than to dissolve the legitimate concerns of liberal theology. Dialectical theology has widened rather than bridged the gap between faith and human experience. It has involuntarily contributed to the present crisis and alienated Christian faith from actual experience of the world. Today, therefore, numerous attempts are made critically to resume the legitimate concerns of the theology of mediation. Nevertheless there is at present great uncertainty about how actually we can introduce

the genuine interests of a theology of mediation into
a critical union of faith and thought, Church and society. The question is: How can we achieve a critical
mediation of faith and thought, Church and society?

1.3 A second Enlightenment

We have arrived at a decisive point in the present
crisis in theology. This crisis is not only apparent in
theology. It exists in the context of a much more inclusive unheaval in the very foundations of modern
society. Somehow or other all three currents which
moulded the intellectual countenance of modern times
are now exhausted. The immanent difficulties of all of
them have become apparent; they no longer work. To
be sure we are still concerned with basic questions
raised by the Enlightenment: the relations between
reason and history, between freedom and authority,
and between the Church and modern society. Yet there
are hardly any clear new perspectives on the future.
Therefore our intellectual life has been overlaid with
a certain langour and resignation. Everywhere there
are trails and searches, but nowhere can we find any
really convincing new approaches.

   At best we can describe the present situation as a
period of a second Enlightenment.[13] The second Enlightenment amounts to an enlightenment of enlightenment about itself, a meta-criticism of its
criticism. It then becomes clear that the Enlightenment was not so free from unconditioned presuppositions as it thought, but was inspired by a belief in
reason and freedom that nowadays seems somewhat
naive. For us today human freedom is anything but
obvious. It is a highly problematic matter. We know

that in many respects we are predetermined psycho-
logically, sociologically and biologically.

We know that reason never begins at zero point, but
that even the very question of reason and the freedom
to reason is an historically moulded problem which
conditions the entire history of the Christian West.
Finally we have to ask: Are we really free at all? Is
trust in reason at all reasonable in itself? The idealistic faith in universal rationality and in universally
pervasive ideas has basically disappeared as a result
of the experience of the twentieth century. Therefore
the second Enlightenment is essentially more prudent
and reserved than the first. It reminds us of the fundamentally finite nature of man. It is profoundly aware
of the relativity and facticity of reality, and of the
transience of all our ideas and conceptual models.

The new experience of man's finiteness, of the
bounds to his reason and of the problematic nature of
his freedom, does not lead directly to a new openness
about the complex of problems relating to religion. On
the contrary, insight into human limitations has persuaded neo-positivists and critical rationalists that
metaphysical and religious questions raised hitherto
are to be rejected from the start as meaningless. The
charge of meaninglessness enables them considerably
to undercut the whole religious question. Instead, the
inclination is to turn to limited, solvable problems and
to avoid all actual or supposed ideological claims to
consider things in the absolute. 'Wovon man nicht
sprechen kann, darüber muss man schweigen' –
'Whereof one cannot speak, thereof one must be silent'
or 'What we cannot speak about we must pass over in
silence'.[14] Wittgenstein's categorical judgment is often
cited nowadays. But with this very proposition Wittgenstein exceeds the bounds of his own postulate. He
too acknowledges a realm of the mystical and inex-

pressible. For how is man able to define his limitations if he does not 'know' about something, in some form or another, that lies beyond the bounds he claims to recognize? Is it not characteristic of man to think, dream and strive beyond the *status quo*, the existent?

The basic problem of the second Enlightenment is accordingly the question of the conditions of freedom. On the one hand, man in his freedom is greater than reality; he exceeds all externally posited bounds. On the other hand, reality is greater than man; it restricts and confines him; indeed, it threatens his freedom. Pascal described the nature of this dialectic.[15] Even though we are unfree, we realize that we are unfree and suffer from our unfreedom. That is the greatness and misery of mankind. The greatness of man is that he recognizes his misfortune; but his misery is that he suffers from his greatness. The fundamental experience of man in this second Enlightenment is therefore the experience of the greatness and misery of mankind. It is the experience of a tension between a transcendence in striving towards which man constantly exceeds himself, and a merciless confinement within the facticity of the existing order of things; between the being and the meaning of the world. In this situation man experiences most poignantly the question of the meaning of his existence and of reality altogether. How under such conditions can man come to terms with himself and his world? How is he to discover a happy and fulfilled existence?

I cannot develop the problem of meaning any further here. Even less can I indicate how it might become once again a way of meaningfully positing the problem of belief. At this point it is a matter of discerning the intellectual, spiritual and social situation of faith today. This is a critical situation, for the traditional approaches to, aids to understanding, and forms of articulating belief are largely redundant. To be sure, this is not a hopeless state of affairs. Initially at least, we can sense new possibilities of talking responsibly about God. Man in his quest for happiness, fulfilment and meaning – in short, man in his search for the humanity of his human nature – is the ground for this hope. Yet this quest of man for himself and for the humanity of his human nature is also a challenge to proclamation and to theology. Do preaching and theology offer any convincing answer to this quest and question of mankind? Seldom has so much been expected of Christian faith as today. Hence the disillusionment and frustration are all the greater if we offer stones instead of bread. And so we may say that the files of the faith question are in no way closed. We are merely at the beginning of a new chapter. The question is whether we intend to accept the challenge and, instead of looking through the pages of past records, are ready to look ahead. This book is offered as a humble effort in that direction.

Notes

1. On the history of the term and concept 'death of God', see G. Hasenhüttl, 'Die Wandlung des Gottesbildes', in : *Theologie im Wandel* (Munich & Freiburg, 1967), pp. 228–53; J. Bishop, *God-is-dead Theology* (London, 1965).
2. Cf. Karl Rahner, 'Kleine Frage zum heutigen Plualismus in der gestigen Situation der Katholiken und der Kirche', in: *Schriften zur Theologie* VI (Einsiedeln & Cologne, 1965), pp. 34–45 (*Theological Investigations*, vol. VI); *id.*, 'Pluralism in Theology and the Unity of Belief in the Church', in: Concilium 5 (1969), 462–6; P. Lengsfeld & I. Hermann, *Die Alternative zum Terror, Pluralismus in Theologie und Kirche* (Düsseldorf, 1970).
3. Cf. Ernst Cassirer, *The Philosophy of the Enlightenment* (Princeton, 1951); P. Hazard, *The European Mind, 1680–1715* (Harmondsworth, 1964); *id., European Thought in the Eighteenth*

Century: From Montesquieu to Lessing (London, 1954); M. Hork-heimer & T. Adorno, *Dialectic of Enlightenment* (New York, 1972; London, 1973); M. Horkheimer, *Eclipse of Reason* (London & New York, 1947); W. Anz, M. Greiner & W. Maurer, 'Aufklärung', in: *RGG*, I³ (1957), pp. 703–50; W. Olmüller, *Die unbefriedigte Auf-klärung* (Frankfurt am Main, 1969); G. Rohrmoser, *Emanzipation und Freiheit* (Munich, 1970); K. Aner, *Die Theologie der Lessing-zeit* (Halle, 1929); K. Barth, *Protestant Theology in the Nineteenth Century* (London, 1972); E. Hirsch, *Geschichte der neueren evan-gelischen Theologie in Zusammenhang mit den allgemeinen Bew-egungen des europäischen Denkens*, vols. 1–5 (Gütersloh, 1949–54); W. Müller, 'Kirchliche Wissenschaft im 18. Jahrhundert – Aufklärungstheologie und Pietismus', in: *Handbuch der Kirchen-geschichte*, Vol. V, ed. H. Jedin (Freiburg im Breisgau, 1970), pp. 571–97; A. Richardson, *The Bible and the Age of Science* (London, 1961); G. R. Cragg, *Reason and Authority in the Eight-eenth Century* (Cambridge, 1964); R. N. Stromberg, *Religious Lib-eralism in Eighteenth-century England* (London, 1954); B. Willey, *The Seventeenth Century Background* (London, 1934); *id., The Eighteenth Century Background* (London, 1940).

4. Immanuel Kant, 'Beantwortung der Frage: Was ist Auf-klärung?', in: *Werke*, ed. W. Weischedel, VI (Darmstadt, 1964), p. 53.

5. Cf., F. Gogarten, *Verhängnis und Hoffnung der Neuzeit. Die Säkularisierung als theologisches Problem* (Stuttgart, 1953); J. B. Metz, *Theology of the World* (London & New York, 1968); *id., Faith in History and Society* (New York & London, 1980); H. Lübbe, *Säkularisierung* (Freiburg, 1965); H. Cox, *The Secular City* (New York & London, 1965).

6. *Pastoral Constitution on the Church in the Modern World (Gaudium et Spes)* No. 36, 56; *Declaration on Religious Freedom (Dignitatis humanae)*. But see Vatican I: *DS* 3019 = *NR* 47.

7. On the discussion of this point see Gogarten, *op. cit.*; J. B. Metz, *Theology of the World, op. cit.*; K. Löwith, *Weltgeschichte und Heilgeschehen* (Stuttgart, ⁴1961); H. Blumenberg, *Legitimität der Neuzeit* (Frankfurt am Main, 1966); G. Rohrmoser, *Emanzi-pation und Freiheit* (Munich, 1970), pp. 9–29.

8. See F. Nietzsche, *Die fröhliche Wissenschaft* (The Happy Science), in *Werke*, ed. K. Schlechta, vol. II (Munich, 1955), p. 127.

9. R. Spaemann, *Der Ursprung der Soziologie aus dem Geist der Restauration* (Munich, 1959); K. Hecker, 'Restoration', in *Sa-cramentum Mundi*, vol. IV (London & New York, 1969).

10. J. R. Geiselmann, *Die Katholische Tübinger Schule* (Freiburg, 1964).

11. G. E. Lessing, 'Brief an seinen Bruder Karl vom 2 Februar 1774', in: *Gesammelte Werke*, IX (Berlin, 1957), p. 597.

12. Karl Marx, *Zur Kritik der Hegelschen Rechtsphilosophie* (On the Critique of the Hegelian Philosophy of Right) in: *Werke-Schriften-Briefe*, I (Darmstadt, 1962), p. 488; *id., Selected Writings in Sociology and Social Philosophy*, eds. T. B. Bottomore & M. Rubel (Harmondsworth, 1963), p. 41.

13. A critique of the notion of the self-positing and self-grounding subject is already to be found in Kant and Hegel; the upheaval which led to the recognition of the pre-existence and facticity of subjectivity exists in varying forms in the late philosophy of Fichte and Schelling. The breakthrough of this insight in Feuerbach, Marx, Kierkegaard and Nietzsche is characteristic of our post-idealistic age. See W. Kasper, *Das Absolute in der Geschichte* (Mainz, 1965). Today the meta-criticism of the modern era is to be found in diverse forms in the most disparate thinkers, for instance: Romano Guardini, *Das Ende der Neuzeit* (Würzburg, 1950); Martin Heidegger, *Der Satz vom Grund* (Pfullingen, 1957); Hans-Georg Gadamer, *Truth and Method* (London, 1975); G. Picht, *Wahrheit-Vernunft-Verantwortung* (Stuttgart, 1969); Theodor W. Adorno, *Zur Metakritik der Erkenntnistheorie* (Stuttgart, 1956); Jürgen Habermas, *Knowledge and Human Interests* (London, 1972); *id., Theory and Practice* (Boston, 1973).

14. Ludwig Wittgenstein, *Tractatus Logico-philosophicus* (London, 1961), p. 74.

15. Blaise Pascal, *[Pascal's] Pensées*, ed. H. F. Stewart (London, 1950).

2 The location of faith

2.1 The relevance of natural theology

We have all met people who seem to go quite dead when we talk about God. In the present situation, it is possibly one of the most severe challenges to believers (at least to those who have to preach the faith) that there is an increasing number of people who lead a happy and fulfilled human life without any belief in God. They seem to lack nothing that faith could give them. At least, faith in the forms and formulas we use to articulate in the Church no longer fits their problems and experiences. But believers too are increasingly oppressed by a feeling that there is a gulf between faith and experience.

In his everyday life the believer finds even fewer traces of God, and verifies his belief less and less often in his daily experience. His faith is like money that is no longer backed up by the hard currency of human experience. This worrying dichotomy between faith and human experience is so pervasive that faith threatens to become a mere superstructure. Therefore one of theology's most urgent concerns must be to restore this 'location in actual life' (or *Sitz im Leben*, as German theologians call it) to faith, and to apply itself to the theme of faith and experience. Although the horizon of the question has changed, this means addressing oneself to the problem of what we might call the natural 'access-point' of faith.

The question of the location of faith in human life is of course far from obvious in theological terms. One might ask whether faith is not a non-deducible gift of grace? Is it possible to verify it against experience or demonstrate it with proofs of the existence of God? Surely faith is something that dissolves in the face of such proofs. . . . A faith that one could prove would no longer be faith. Anyone who tries to prove too much in this regard, proves too little. And, finally, is not the experience of the distance and absence of God an indication of the self-alienation of the sinner? Surely, then, faith cannot fit so neatly the actual or supposed axioms of our experience? Such questions have often been posed by Protestant theology, especially since the theological renaissance introduced by Karl Barth.

In his early phase, especially, Barth found as follows: God is God; he is the quite Other, the Hidden and Mysterious. It would be presumptous, pride indeed, if man were to imagine that he could recognize God by his own human power. God can be known only by God. God can be conceived only in the obedience of faith, if God offers himself to be known through his revelation. Catholic circles have never fully accepted this radical form of the theology of revelation. It has not yielded to another, Catholic understanding of the relation between God and the world, between grace and human nature, and to another, Catholic notion of sin. But in connection with the biblical and kerygmatic renewal, a theology of the word and of proclamation did emerge within Catholicism which constantly referred to Pascal's famous dictum that faith was not a matter of the God of the philosophers but of the God of Abraham, Isaac and Jacob,[1] of the God who is the Father of Jesus Christ.

This theology of the word is a wholly understandable reaction against a philosophically alien neo-scholasticism, and against a far too reductive accommodation of faith and experience in liberalism and Modernism. We should lose substantially were we to try to return to a situation before the renewal movements of the first half of this century. Nevertheless we do have to recover the legitimate concerns of natural theology,[2] and to a certain extent of liberal theology and of Modernism, whose problems were more frozen than solved at the beginning of the century. A purely biblical theology and proclamation grounded only on the word accord neither with Catholic tradition nor with an appropriate theological understanding of faith. Faith is a fully and wholly human act in spite of all non-indebtedness and bestowal of grace. It is a man who believes and not the Holy Spirit in man. As a human act, however, belief may not be an arbitary decision. It has to be acknowledged as something humanly meaningful and as something intellectually honourable and responsible. If it were anything else it would be unworthy of God and of man. For that reason, faith must not be a pious transcendence of the world. Any such, even apparent, 'pure' faith would be mere flight from reality; sooner or later it would be exposed as empty and unreal.

Therefore in preaching it is not enough to bombard people with kerygmatic and dogmatic formulas and to say: 'Eat, bird or die'.[3] Our notion of faith is false if we merely repeat constantly that this person or that no longer believes this or that tenet of faith, or even if we only ask cynically: Are you leaving too? Theology and proclamation have to be missionary in a true sense; that is, they have to interpret the articles of faith in such a way that they are comprehensible in actual human situations; so that they are a genuine challenge to people, and a demand that a decision should be made. It is not enough to harrass the formal authority of God or of the Church, but it is a question of allowing room for a mature decision of faith. But that is possible only if we allow a decision of faith its proper place in human experience. Without such a point of access, without an access that is commensurate with human experience, all other theological arguments are irrelevant. Without this existential location they are without any living power; they turn abstract and ideological. In other words: precisely because faith makes a universal and unconditioned claim, it has to discover God in all things, as the medieval mystics said. When people talk nowadays of 'immanent transcendence' and a 'secular' faith, often the same thing is meant. There is no theology from above that does not complement a theology from below.

Of course it is possible to establish faith in experience erroneously and with wrong effect. But that is possible only if we reduce faith to experiential phenomena which are solely anthropological and sociological. It is also possible if we remove faith entirely to the realm of the supernatural and the beyond, so that it loses all contact with our reality here and now. This latter danger has proved especially acute in the modern age. Insofar as human knowledge has pushed further and further ahead to reveal the natural bases of reality, faith has been increasingly entangled in skirmishing actions on a retreat road. Repeated attempts have been made to locate God in the gaps of knowledge as it happens to be at a particular time. But that has made him the 'God of the gaps', and has reduced God to a gap-filler and to a hypothesis, to an explanation of phenomena that have not yet been accorded a natural explanation. For the most part all

such positions have had to be abandoned very quickly
in the face of the advance of science, and new outposts
have had to be set up. Hence the reality of God has
shifted increasingly beyond 'natural' experience. God
has become increasingly unworldly, and the world increasingly Godless. But this God of the gaps is not God
but an idol. He is no longer the universal Lord of all
reality, but human wish-fulfilment and a mere aid to
human self-realization. The God of the gaps is called
in when our Latin no longer covers the situation. Then
God is degraded to the status of a means, to the level
of a means conceptually to appropriate mastery of reality. Therefore we must say that the God-question is
possible only within a universally speculative horizon.
In other words, we can talk meaningfully of God only
if we do not ask about this or that fact or phenomenon
or aspect, and only if we are really concerned with the
question of the meaning of all reality. Therefore the
question of meaning is the approach to a comprehensible and responsible discussion of God.

2.2 The question of meaning as the question of God

Then of course we have to ask: are men today still
interested in the question of the meaning[4] of life and of
reality as a whole? There are philosophical currents
which treat this question, because it is unanswerable,
as inherently meaningless. Remember Wittgenstein's
categorical: 'Whereof we cannot speak, thereof we
must remain silent'.[5] Does that mean that we have to
restrict ourselves to special instances of meaning, to
specific soluble problems, and have to avoid the inso-
luble questions of religion and metaphysics?

It may be intellectually responsible to adopt such a

position, but is it really possible in practice? Is it possible to ignore the question of meaning at certain focal points of one's life? To be sure one can force it out of one's conscious mind. But in practice everyone lives by reference to a meaningful model of things. Everyone has a specific idea of what he means by a happy and fulfilled life, and everyone suffers when he no longer finds any meaning in what he does. The absence of meaning often leads to the most severe mental illnesses. Hence, negatively speaking, no one can live without a certain answer to the question of meaning. Perhaps he or she does not speak of meaning, but what else does anyone have in mind when seeking for happiness, love and fulfilment? In all these instances an individual is looking for harmony between self and world, and for harmony between world and self. That is what we call meaning. There is meaning where the world becomes a human world: a just, peaceful human world, with which man can identify. Meaning is what we call a healthy and whole existence of man in and with his world.

Positively speaking, the inescapability of the question of meaning can be shown if we address ourselves to anthropology. Man is distinct from an animal in that he is not fixed by means of instinctual responses in a predetermined environment. The human environment is reality as a whole. Hence man is characterized by his openness to the world. But that also means that he is exposed and unprotected. First he must build his environment. Man is that which is proposed to and thrown upon self. Human existence is always offering and always labour. We are all human beings by right of birth, and yet every day we have to exert ourselves to live as humane human beings. Therefore man himself must also project and construct the location and meaning of his own existence. Hence the question of meaning is directly posited with the dignity of man. An abandonment of the question of meaning would imply an abandonment of the humanity of man. The proclamation of faith constantly raises this question and confronts us with it; in this respect alone it is of service to man.

The question of the meaning of human life is wholly characteristic of man. However, the way in which this question is put can change according to time and place. We may divide the question of universal meaning into the following three phases.

Classical and medieval metaphysics asked about the meaning of reality when they inquired into the ultimate ground of that which is. The basic question of metaphysics is: Why is there anything at all, and not nothing? In the course of this inquiry metaphysicians arrived at the postulate of an ultimate, all-causing, absolute cause that was in itself the cause of its own causation. This primal cause was then equated with the God of revelation. For people of modern times this cosmologico-ontological method (quite apart from what one might think of its philosophical acceptability) is no longer commensurate with experience. Since modern man has no longer been able simply to accept his world as a pregiven reality, but has constructed it himself, he finds God's tracks increasingly less often than his own in the world. Because of our modern technological and industrial civilization we no longer live primarily in a pristine reality but in secondary and tertiary worlds which man himself has made. In modern times, therefore, the problem of meaning has shifted. Insofar as man has made the external world the mere material of his freedom, he is thrown back on himself whenever the question of meaning is raised. Insofar as he has made himself the reference-point of reality, the question that has to be asked is the question of the meaning of his own existence. Man has increasingly discovered the depths of his own soul, the values of his personality; he has sought God in his conscience, in his feelings, and in the transcendental orientation of his spirit and of his freedom. God has been discovered as a profound dimension of man, as the correlate of his own infinity and as a postulate of his freedom (Kant).

Yet this road too has proved problematic. Feuerbach tried to expose this way of knowing God as a mere projection of human longings. Surely, he claimed, in so doing man projected onto the image of an absolute subject his own infinity or his own longing for the infinite. . . . Surely at the end of this road all that man finds is himself. . . . Is this God anything more than mere wish-fulfilment, a substitute? A second objection was raised against the anthropological approach. Marx asked: Is there such a thing as 'man'? And he answered: Man does in fact 'exist' but only in his actual physical and social relations. We can also say that there is such a thing as man only within human history. Then the question of meaning arises only in an historical context. It is concerned not only with the meaning of each human individual, but with the meaning of man in history. Hence the anthropological approach, at least in the form developed by existentialism in the twentieth century, is not and cannot be inclusive enough.

Criticism of the cosmologico-metaphysical approach,and of the anthropologico-personal approach, shows us the direction we have to take nowadays in answering the question of meaning. We can prescind neither solely from the pregiven reality of nature, nor solely from the nature of man. We encounter the world only as it is historically changed and determined by men, culture and civilization; just as, *vice versa*, man is moulded by socio-cultural factors. Hence we can pose the problem of meaning only in an historical perspective. By 'history' in this respect we understand the abovementioned reciprocal meditation and inter-penetration of world and man: that ongoing process in which man realizes himself by realizing the potential-ities which are pregiven in reality. This historical real-ity is never finished; it is a continually open process. Everything in it is constantly reforming and ferment-ing. Everything is constantly at stake. Everything is a venture. In an historical world new aspects and steps forward constantly interest us. But it is also a world of crises, where nothing is stable. Man constantly wav-ers between hope and fear of the future. History is a constant up-and-down, an unending to-and-fro. That forces man to pose the question of meaning in a new and very urgent way. How are we to understand his-tory? As eternal recurrence? As a history of recession or as a history of progess? Is it on its way into the void, or does it come to rest in a state of fulfilment and completion?

The place where the question of meaning is posed in a world that has been formed historically, is the question of the future. At present man is not in any sort of world with which he can simply identify. There-fore he can only hope for a meaningful, just, human world from the future. The question of what such a meaningful world will be like cannot be answered by scientific and technological means alone. Science and technology can be used only to answer questions with-in an ends-means context. Science can help us to de-cide what means are needed in order to reach a specific goal, and with the aid of technology we can try to prepare those means. But science and technology can-not declare what the right ends are. Even futurology can only extrapolate already existing possibilities and tendencies; but it cannot say which of those possibilities are meaningful for men and for human society. The question of the meaning of man and of social evolution as a whole circumscribes individual scientific problems. Therefore it cannot be treated in the same way as individual scientific conundrums.

It is impossible to conceive the whole, the all-inclusive, in the same way as one conceives a particular element of that whole. It includes us too. We too are at a venture. Here we cannot make a neutral but only a committed judgment. Here each man or woman believes in his or her own way. That does not mean that the question of meaning can be left arbitrarily to the choice of each individual. Here, where mankind itself is in question, the greatest possible precision of thought is required. Therefore, as in the past, we resort to the human or cultural sciences, which differ methodologically from the natural sciences. It is the task of the human sciences to address themselves to men's questions about meaning and to offer them meaningful possibilities for the planning of the future.

2.3 The God-question today

The decisive question for us is whether there is any room for theology within this kind of future-oriented reality: room for meaningful and responsible talk about God.[6] At first sight that space would seem already to be occupied. Transcendence upwards would seem to have been replaced by a form of transcendence ahead – transcendence into an infinitely open future. Many atheists too, and especially many younger Marxist philosophers, recognize this kind of transcendence – a constant self-surpassing human movement forwards into a new, better and more just future.

But this transcendence ahead is not the same as transcendence as Christians understand it. Transcendence ahead is a challenge to human activity; transcendence above, on the other hand, means hope in grace. It would be tantamount to a short-circuit simply to convert Christian faith into a revolutionary force in the service of a better and more just future order of society. The biblical God is not always on the side of the bigger battalions and of those who are building the future. He is also – he is precisely – the God of those who fall too short, of the little people, and of those who are so poor and so weak that they make no revolution and can contribute nothing to social progress. And when he promises precisely such a peripheral future, then his must obviously be a future other than that which is no more than an extension of things already potential and latent in reality. The God who estalished the future on the cross promises a hope against all hope (Rom. 4: 18). Precisely by transcending the ungraced nature of our achievement-orientated planning for the future, he shows himself to be the God of mankind and the God of a human future in which we shall be able against all hope to trust in meaning. The future of God as professed by Christian faith is therefore not only a future from below (*futurum*), but a real state of things to come: a future which is outside human projection and manipulation, and which approaches us without deduction and derivation (*adventum*).[7]

We may look at the question of this Christian future in two aspects:

The first approach begins with the experience of injustice, hatred and lies in history. We experience history not only as the history of progress, but just as much as the history of suffering – as an immense road of human misery. Injustice and suffering are usually

the strongest objections to belief in God; they are existentially deeper and more powerful than all purely
conceptual difficulties. How are we to believe that an
almighty and omniscient God is the loving Father of
mankind, if he permits Auschwitz? Such questions are
not easily argued away. The experience of injustice
and suffering implies yet another: even if we ourselves
are err a hundred times, we cannot be satisfied with
a world in which some die of hunger while others
suffer from the consequences of their well-being. Evil
evokes the judgment that it just can't go on like that.
We have to protest. And in that protest there is something unconditioned and no longer questionable. Unless we want to surrender our very humanity, our
selves, we cannot doubt that it is wrong to kill an
innocent child, that it is wrong to torture people. Injustice and suffering cry out for absolute justice. Injustice and lies can and must not be the ultimate truth.
The question is undeniably: How are we to go any
further?

The powers of evil affect every one of us. No one can
wholly evade them and make a unique personal claim
to goodness. With every attempt to build a more just,
more free and more peaceful order, we ourselves are
conditioned by injustice and force. We even have to
use force in order to fight against the unjust use of
force. Therefore we bear into every new order the seeds
of new disorder, new injustice and new discontent. We
can never sever ourselves completely from our past; it
is a constant encumbrance. Clearly we can never escape of our own power from this satanic circle of force
and counter-force, injustice and revenge. Is there,
then, nothing left in the end but a 'longing for something quite different' (Max Horkheimer)? Or is there
not an injustice that literally cries to heaven for
justice?

If our inalienable and unconquerable hope in a better and more human future is not in vain, and if we are not to despair absolutely of a meaning in history, we have to make a qualitative leap. We have to seize upon something qualitatively new which is in no way deducible from the circumstances of present history: something new that lies beyond human planning and capabilities, something that we can only allow to be given to us. We cannot 'conceive' this quite different and qualitatively new thing, for we live in the circumstances, under the conditions, of the present. We cannot describe the absolute future in positive anticipations and futuristic utopias. We 'possess' it only in the form of what might be called a 'negative mediation' and in the way offered by hope. Hence the question of the meaning of our existence and of our location in history is indeed a possible means of access to the God to whom the Scriptures testify as the God of hope (Rom. 15:3). Yet it is not as though we could prove the existence of God in this way. Nevertheless God's message is a meaningful project for a meaningful human existence. The non-biblical category of meaning proves to be a translation of what the Bible calls 'promise'.[8]

A second attempt to find a point of access to a comprehensible way of talking about God begins with a more profound experience of man wherever that is possible. Injustice and suffering may be understood as historically produced, and therefore as historically responsible and also – to a certain extent – historically alterable forms of human alienation from a meaningful human existence. In addition to such forms of historical alienation, there is however what we might call the 'metaphysical alienation' of man; metaphysical, because it is constitutively posited in man's existence as a human being: the experience of human finiteness. To be sure, our experience is that with his freedom man transcends all that is given. But we also experience the fact that reality is bigger than man. We always fall foul of that. We are always experiencing our limitations. We can never quite master reality. Every attempt to control the whole (*totum*) necessarily becomes totalitarian.

 Our clearest and most drastic experience of the finiteness of humanity and of its plans for the future is in regard to death. At this point all futuristic utopias grounded within history collapse. And here the question of meaning is posed with ultimate force. What is the value of human life and creativity? Do they ultimately vanish into the void and collapse into nullity? Where is everything heading in the end? Must we as finite beings finally surrender hope in any ultimate meaning and rest content with our limited experience? Can we as finite beings really grasp the infinite without failing to grasp it? Does it as far as we are concerned have to remain something absolutely alien and alienating? Can it mean something other than the absolutely closed mystery of experience which, as it were, offers us from its great distance a great big ultimate snub? Is it in the end no more than an abstract and absurd term for the absurdity of existence? These questions show that it would be inadequate merely to equate human longing and the human thrust towards the infinite with God – as often happens. For the time being it must remain an open question what this infinite is – God or nothingness.

Yet here too, as with the first approach, a second experience becomes manifest. It too is indissolubly connected with the experience of finiteness. In order to lead a human life we have to assume that life has a meaning. In spite of all limiting experiences, we nevertheless constantly have to live this life we are in. Hence the experience of finiteness implies the experience of a 'nevertheless' and a 'yet again'. Against the background of the very threat of nothingness and the absurd we constantly experience the fact that things have a certain solidity; that there are good times and good encounters; in short, that 'it is worth it'. Precisely because happiness is not obvious, we are able to experience happiness as happiness. The fact that there is meaning is not to be deduced in the form of a mere 'pro-jection'; it is much more the inalienable presupposition of life.

Such meaning cannot be derived from finiteness, if we are to take seriously the question posed by nothingness. It is experienced as undeducible, as underivable, as chance and as a gift. The experience of meaning has therefore to be interpreted as the experience of transcendence. Only thus is it possible to do justice to both experiences: that of the non-availability and that of the givenness of meaning. Because of the finiteness of man we have to say: 'It is pointless to try to preserve the notion of an unconditioned meaning without God'.[9] Only if God is, only if the God who – because he is the creator of reality – controls the conditions of reality as a whole which are beyond man's reach is, can it be meaningful to trust in an absolute meaning.[10] Only God as the Lord of all reality can overcome the alienation which is given with finiteness, and only he can also guarantee a future beyond death. Only the God who the Scriptures say is the God who makes the dead to live (Rom. 4:17; 2 Cor. 1:9) can support the meaning of our existence. Only he can be an assurance for the hope that what we have done will not be lost in the void but will be included in the ultimate condition of reality – even though in a way that we cannot conceive in any detail.

To summarize: We began with the question of how

we today can postulate belief in God in an intellectually responsible and honourable way. We have not
offered any proof of the existence of God. That is forbidden us, not least of all by the experience of suffering
and of human limitations. The experience of meaninglessness has to be taken just as seriously as the signs
and traces of meaning. Therefore we can posit absolute
meaning only in the form of hope. Such hope is inseparable from human life. The alternative could only
be despair and suicide, or absolute indifference: 'Let
us eat and drink for tomorrow we die' (1 Cor. 15:32).
Hence there remains only the hope that meaning and
not meaninglessness, that justice and not injustice,
that truth and not lies, that happiness and not nameless suffering will prove to be the ultimate experience
of history. What the Bible and Christian tradition call
'God' shows itself to be an offer and a challenge to
human hope. Therefore it is meaningful to talk of God
as the power of the future, as the future of our projects
for the future, as the power which liberates us and
gives us courage to be human beings. Of course God
could not be the absolute future of history if he were
not also the absolute origin of all reality. To that extent, an historically orientated approach to thought
can and must take up critically and creatively the
questions and concerns of classical metaphysics.

If we talk thus of God as the power of the future, we
do not recast God as a gap-filler. He is not our answer
to this or that particular question, but the answer to
the fundamental human situation. Hence this answer
does not suppress human knowledge and achievement.
God does not deny and mar human happiness. On the
contrary: belief in God allows human searching and
planning its ultimate meaning. A properly conceived
faith in fact provokes seeking and asking. It inspires
human application. Hope in the eschatological future

of God first makes really possible any projects for the future which is established within history. Inasmuch as that hope liberates us from existential anxiety and anguish it sets us free to serve others. That hope does not offer us empty promises but fills us with courage. The objections atheists raise to faith often have to do with mistakes about that faith. Christians have not seldom been guilty of such misunderstanding of the nature of faith. Far too often they have denounced instead of encouraged natural human potential. Therefore we all have reason to treat the queries of modern atheism as a catharsis of our own faith and to pass through it to a more profound and better understanding of belief. But we must also ask the atheist whether he has something better to offer; whether he has an answer which is more appropriate to man and to his quest for meaning. If we ask thus, then the quarrel between belief and unbelief will cease to be a debate about absolute worlds and superworlds. It will become a debate about which attitude, belief or unbelief, is more appropriate to human reality. This debate about man and about his hope in history is just as meaningful today as it was in the past. And here, now as in the past, faith finds its place in our experience of the world.

Notes

1. Cf. Pascal, *op. cit.*
2. On the rehabilitation of the legitimate concern of natural theology within present-day Protestant theology, see G. Ebeling 'Erwägungen zu einer Evangelischen Fundamentaltheologie', in: *ZThK* 67 (1970), pp. 479–524; L. Gilkey in *Concilium* 5 (1969); *id.*, *Naming the Whirlwind. The Renewal of God-language* (Indianapolis & New York, 1969).

3. Dietrich Bonhoeffer, *Letters and Papers from Prison* (London, 1953).

4. On the question of meaning see R. Lauth, *Die Frage nach dem Sinn des Daseins* (Munich, 1953); B. Welte, *Auf der Spur des Ewigen* (Freiburg, 1963); M. Machovec, *Vom Sinn des menschlichen Lebens* (Freiburg, 1971).

5. Ludwig Wittgenstein, *Tractatus Logicus-philosophicus* (London, 1961), p. 74.

6. On the God-question, see among the many available works: Karl Rahner, *Theological Investigations*, Vol. IX (London, 1972); Hans Küng, *Being a Christian* (London & New York, 1977); E. Schillebeeckx, *Jesus Christ* (London, 1978); E. Jüngel, *Gottes Sein ist im Werden* (Tübingen, 1965); H. Zahrnt, *Die Sache mit Gott* (Munich, 1961); *id., Gott kann nicht sterben* (Munich, 1970); John Robinson, *Honest to God* (London, 1963); Hans Küng, *Does God Exist?* (New York & London, 1980).

7. Cf. J. Moltmann, 'Antwort auf die Kritik an der Theologie der Hoffnung', in *Diskussion über die 'Theologie der Hoffnung'*, ed. W.-D. Marsch (Munich, 1967), pp. 210ff.

8. See D. Bonhoeffer, *Letters and Papers from Prison* (London, 1953).

9. Max Horkheimer, *Die Sehnsucht nach dem ganz Anderen* (Hamburg, 1970), p. 69.

10. This line of argument includes a point from Kant's *Critique of Practical Reason*.

3 Jesus Christ: the witness to faith

3.1 The failure of the quest for the historical Jesus

All that I have said so far about the justification of faith has been confined to some extent to preliminary observations. I have spoken of various signs and indications that might lead to the situation in which faith is possible. The question concerning the meaning of the whole of our reality seemed, for example, to be a possible location of faith, but the signs pointing to such an ultimate meaning were vague and ambiguous. There were, however, signs pointing not to an unconditional meaning, but to the ultimate absurdity of reality, and I therefore concluded that an ultimate absence of ambiguity was not possible in this sphere. For Christians, the sign of God in this world, the sign that gives certainty to all other signs and deprives them of their ambiguity, is Jesus Christ. He is the sign of and the witness to faith. All attempts to justify faith must therefore be based on him. Christian faith stands or falls with him.

This argument gives rise to a number of questions. Have the historical figure of Jesus and the form of his message not, for example, been made extremely vague because of the historical and critical method of exegesis? Are there not so many different and even contradictory interpretations of the person and the work

of Jesus that everything is fundamentally questionable? Has anything more than a heap of fragments been
left behind by the historical and critical examination
of the New Testament? How can such an uncertain
basis be used as the point of departure for an attempt
to justify faith?

Because of these and other related questions, we
must go back to the sources before asking about the
person of Jesus and his cause, and find out whether
they can provide us with reliable information.

For centuries Christians were convinced that the
four gospels should be read as faithful historical reports and testimonies of the Church's faith in Jesus
Christ as true man and true God. One of the most
important events in the whole history of theology was
undoubtedly the emergence of the historical and critical method.[1] According to Albert Schweitzer, in his
history of the quest for the historical Jesus, it was the
greatest event in German theology and represented
'the most tremendous aspect that has ever been undertaken in religious thought'. The point of departure in
this historical research into the life of Jesus was not,
Schweitzer was careful to point out, purely an interest
in history. It was fundamentally an attempt to look
for the Jesus of history as a helper in the struggle to
become free from dogma.[2]

According to Schweitzer, the Christology of Chalcedon had overlaid the historical figure of Jesus with
the concepts of Greek philosophy and, in so doing, had
alienated it from modern historical thought. The aim
of the protagonists of the historical and critical method
was therefore to remove the later layers of the paint-
ing and restore the original colour and lustre, in the
conviction that the historical Jesus – Jesus as he really
was – would be more in accordance with modern taste
than the dogmatic Christ of the doctrine of the two

natures. The result would be that each successive period of modern theology ought to be able to discover its ideal in Jesus. Schweitzer in fact sketched out such a long and changing history of research into the life of Jesus, from Hermann Samuel Reimarus in the eighteenth century, David Friedrich Strauss, Friedrich Schleiermacher, Ernest Renan and Adolf von Harnack until the present day. Since nothing is, in principle, impossible in science, Drews and others declared, at about the turn of the present century, that Jesus was not a historical figure at all and was purely mythical, a suggestion that is now only taken seriously in out-of-date Communist text-books.

The history of historical and critical research into the life of Jesus is also at an end now in any theological work that is to be taken seriously. Two data led to the breakdown of an entire period of theology. The first was the recognition that the Jesus of Nazareth, who appeared as the Messiah, proclaimed the morality of the kingdom of God, established the kingdom of heaven on earth and died, never in fact existed.[3] Jesus was not a modern man and he cannot be modernized in any way at all. Anyone who comes closer to him is bound to discover a radical strangeness in him. The most important discovery made by Albert Schweitzer and Johannes Weiss in their historical and critical research into the New Testament was that eschatology was at the heart of Jesus' message.

This eschatology strikes us today as very strange. Schweitzer and Weiss were mistaken in believing that Jesus' eschatological teaching was apocalyptic in that it insisted that the existing world would be completely destroyed and that a new, heavenly world would miraculously descend to replace it. This background of apocalyptic ideas is now no longer attributed to Jesus himself, but is generally believed to go back to a later biblical tradition. Despite this, however, the discovery of the eschatological character of Jesus' message is still valid. This eschatological message of the future of God is nonetheless bound to strike us, whose historical thinking is purely immanent, as mythological, with the result that, for modern secularized man, the person of Jesus himself and his message are inevitably strange.

The second datum was even more important than the first. It is that the gospels do not allow us to write a life of Jesus. They do not provide a biography of Jesus or a psychology of Jesus. They are rather written in the form of historical reports of post-paschal proclamation. This datum is probably the most important insight gained by the leading representatives of the school of form criticism, Martin Dibelius and Rudolf Bultmann, whose methods and results were for a long time seriously criticized. In the case of Bultmann, the reason for this critical rejection is to be found in the Marburg professor's presentation of form criticism in close association with an existential interpretation of the New Testament and his demythologization of the gospels. Form criticism can, however, be practised without this existential interpretation and process of demythologization.

The methods and results of form criticism were also accepted, with some reservations, by the second Vatican Council. In the Council's *Constitution on Revelation*, a distinction was made between three stages of the gospel tradition. The first stage is what Jesus Christ himself did and taught during his earthly life. The second is what the apostles 'handed on ... with that clearer understanding' after the Easter event in the light of the resurrection. The third stage recognized in the *Constitution on Revelation* is that of the editing of the gospels. The evangelists selected, summarized and clarified in accordance with the situation in which the Church was placed, but preserved the form of proclamation.[4] It is clear, then, that the most fundamental insights of form criticism were officially recognized and accepted by the second Vatican Council.

These two data mark the end of theological research into the life of Jesus. From the point of view of systematic theology, however, a number of conclusions can be drawn from them. Many wonderful systematic Christ-roses have certainly been cultivated in the field of historical scepticism.[5] One consequence that has been at least partly drawn from the failure of the quest for the historical Jesus is that we may now safely return to the old channel of dogmatic Christology. Many so-called conservative theologians have taken possession of the 'progressive' exegetical results and have decided to keep strictly to the post-paschal proclamation of the Church, since nothing can be known with historical certainty about Jesus himself. This led to the neo-orthodox movements in twentieth-century theology, in which a remarkable symbiosis between dogmatic theology and modern biblical exegesis has been achieved. It also led to a widely discussed change of fronts, as represented in the theology of Ernst Käsemann. The more clearly certain aspects of the new exegesis were revealed as negative, the more urgently the conservative theologians, who had eventually taken over the liberal theologians' research into the historical Jesus whom they had for so long disputed, had to save what they could from the burning house.

Bultmann himself drew an entirely different conclusion. He made a theological virtue out of the historical necessity. In his opinion, it was not necessary to enquire about the historical Jesus behind the kerygma,

since this would be an attempt to make sure of faith
by objective arguments and therefore fundamentally
a lack of faith. Bultmann declared that he did not
know and did not want to know what had gone in in
Jesus' heart.[6] Only the fact that Jesus had come was
important for him. He was therefore able to combine
a decidedly radical point of view with an equally radical historical scepticism. The value of the figure of
Jesus as a sign, which is precisely what makes faith
possible, was, however, destroyed in Bultmann's
theology.

3.2 The new quest for the historical Jesus

Although Bultmann is already one of the classical
theologians of the twentieth century, he is certainly
not the most modern. In their research into the question of the historical Jesus, the theologians who have
followed Bultmann have not in any way determined
their position. The advances made in this field by
Ernst Käsemann led to a new quest for the historical
Jesus.[7] In his research, Käsemann considered a legitimate concern of the liberal quest for the historical
Jesus within the framework of the changed theological
climate of the second half of the twentieth century.
There were two important reasons for this.

The first is this. Even though it may be impossible
for us to reconstruct a life of Jesus and many of Jesus'
reported words and actions have to be regarded as the
products of post-paschal theology, editorial insertions
and so on, it is not true to say that no more than a
heap of fragments has been left by the earlier liberal
research into the historical Jesus, with the result that
practically nothing more can be said with certainty.
The situation is by no means so confused and hopeless

as many popular publications often rather irresponsibly try to maintain. There is no reason at all for us to give way to radical historical scepticism. As Günter Bornkamm has rightly pointed out, the faith of the Christian community was 'not simply the product of their imagination, but their response to Jesus' figure and mission as a whole'. The gospels do not entitle us to be resigned or sceptical. 'On the contrary, they make the historical figure of Jesus in its direct power visible to us, although they do not do this in the same way as chronicles or histories would do it. It is all too clear what the gospels report about Jesus' message, his actions and his history. They are still marked by authenticity and freshness and also by a special quality which is not dominated by the paschal faith of the early Christian community, but which points directly to the earthly figure of Jesus himself.' Bornkamm thought that the literary genre of the gospels was specific in that they proclaimed their message through history and that they proclaimed by reporting a history. 'It is the theologian's task to look for history in the kerygma of the gospels and also to look for the kerygma in that history.'[8]

This programme leads us to the second concern underlying the new quest for the historical Jesus. Käsemann was conscious of the danger of docetism, in other words, of underestimating and even suppressing Jesus' humanity and its saving significance in theology that neglected the earthly Jesus and placed a one-sided emphasis on the proclaimed Christ. One of the fundamental concerns of the Christology of the early Church was, of course, the human and historical nature of man's redemption. Another danger of which Käsemann was aware in Bultmann's theology was that of an enthusiasm that, in stressing the reality of salvation here and now, is forgetful of the fact that

this salvation originated in the historical event of the
crucifixion and that the Christian lives in the shadow
of the cross until his redemption is fully brought about
at the end of time. What is forgotten, then, in this new
research into the life of Jesus is that, although Jesus
is made present in the Church and its proclamation,
Christ does not become merged into the Church, but
remains Lord of that Church. The priority of Jesus
Christ means that the Church's word cannot simply
be identified with the word of Christ. The Church is
rather tied to its criterion that has already been provided in Christ. The quest for the historical Jesus
should express this priority of Christ over the Church.
It should show that Jesus is the beginning, the constant ground and the norm of faith. The most important question that has to be answered, then, is : Who
was this Jesus of Nazareth? Equally important questions are: What was the content of his message and
what did he have to say about himself?

3.3 The message of the kingdom of God

Jesus can best be understood by considering his behaviour. There can be no doubt that he carried out all
the duties of a pious Jew, praying and taking part in
the services at the synagogue and the Temple. He was
not, however, pious in the sense in which piety was
then and is now generally understood. He was pious
in an unprecedented and even revolutionary way,
which pious men of his period found scandalizing and
blasphemous. He was not ascetic. He shared the ban-
quets of rich men and was therefore criticized as a
glutton and a drinker (Mt 11:19). What is more, he did
not observe the laws of cultic purity (Mk 7:1–23), he
broke the commandment to keep the sabbath (Mk

JESUS CHRIST: THE WITNESS TO FAITH   45

2:23–28) and associated with tax-collectors, prostitutes and sinners (Mk 7: 13–17), in other words, with all those who led a marginal existence. He broke the sacred conventions of religion and society. Man, not the law, was the norm of authentic piety for Jesus. 'The sabbath was made for man, not man for the sabbath' (Mk 2:27) sums up his attitude. He therefore provoked the representatives of the religious establishment of the time and goaded them into opposition.

On the other hand, it would be quite wrong to regard Jesus as a political revolutionary in the usual sense of the word. One of the most remarkable aspects of his whole attitude is revealed in the fact that he was never a zealot, opposing the established religious and political powers with force. At the very centre of Jesus' moral attitude and teaching was not violence of a kind that gave rise to further violence in return, but love. Jesus did not want to wound, but to heal wounds. He put an end to the unhappy circle of violence and counter-violence with his commandment to love one's enemies (Mt 5.38–48). He called for a renunciation of violence and his own way was one of suffering, from which violence was strikingly absent.

This attitude indirectly had social consequences, since Jesus was a revolutionary in a much deeper sense than that which is usually given to the word.[9] He was in the last resort diametrically opposed to all existing norms. He called for nothing less than a total conversion, not only of external structures and forms of behaviour, but also of man's heart itself and his fundamental orientation.

The unprecedented freedom that appeared with Jesus gave rise to the question: 'By what authority are you doing these things?' (Mk 11:28). What was the ground and centre of Jesus' being? The only possible answer was and is that Jesus had the power and inspiration to act with such unprecedented freedom from what he proclaimed as the coming of the kingdom of God. According to Käsemann, 'fellow-humanity was the sphere in which his gospel lived, not its foundation or its objective'.[10] The freedom with which Jesus promised salvation to sinners and outcasts calls for a justification and this can be found in the kingdom of God, which formed the centre of his message and the real content of his existence (Mk 1:14f).

Almost all biblical exegetes agree that the kingdom of God is not a kingdom or rule in the sense in which we usually understand the term. It is not a political order based on theocracy. On the contrary, it does away with all human claims to domination, because it is based on a concept of rule that is outside the reach of man and reserved for God alone (Mk 13:32). The kingdom of God cannot be reduced to an historical status. According to Jesus' message, it comes like lightning (Mt 24:27). We cannot know how it comes (Mk 4:26–29). It is the rule of God himself, the manifestation of his divinity, the establishment of his law and justice and at the same time the quintessence of man's deepest expectation of salvation.

Whenever man forgoes care for his own salvation and trusts in God, he escapes from the inhuman pressure of the need to achieve and from anxiety, and becomes joyful. That is why joy is an essential gift of the coming of the kingdom of God. Wholeness and salvation are only possible when man is set free from historical and other purposes. The manifestation of God's divinity and the gift of man's humanity are therefore two sides of the same coin. As the Roman Missal puts it, *Deo servire regnare est*. The kingdom and rule of God mean that God makes his cause man's cause, and man's cause his own.

God's rule cannot be organized either in a revolutionary or in an evolutionary and conservative way. The only preparation that man can make for its coming is to give up his fundamental orientation towards ruling and possessing the world and finding security for himself, and in this way to create a space for God as the only reliable safeguard. What is required of him is a radically new orientation. He has to be converted. Conversion is the negative expression of what Jesus positively called faith. Faith implies a recognition of God's divinity. This recognition is practical and concrete whenever man builds on God as his foundation. Faith is not an achievement. On the contrary, it is a renunciation of all achievement, a state of being empty for God so that we can be completely filled with him. Faith, then, is the concrete way in which the kingdom of God can be present in man. God is Lord whenever he is believed in as Lord and obeyed as Lord. The kingdom of God and faith are therefore two sides of the same coin. The coming of the kingdom of God means that God makes himself valid in man's recognition and faith.

This concentration of Jesus' message on faith does not imply a reduction to a purely inner and spiritual message. All Jesus' miraculous actions bear witness to the fact that his message of the coming of the kingdom of God is concerned with man as a whole in all his physical and social relationships.[12] Not only from the point of view of the natural sciences, but also in the historical sense, these actions undoubtedly present us with a very difficult problem today. There is, however, general agreement among exegetes in that they hardly dispute the historical existence of certain basic miraculous actions, especially the healings and the cases in which demons were driven out. In addition to this, these actions are also too closely associated with certain statements made by Jesus that are regarded as authentic. (An example of this is to be found in Lk 11:20). If it were not for this, it would hardly be possible to explain how the later tradition of miracles was possible. In any case, these actions are not strictly miraculous – they are signs. They had the aim of leading men to faith and can, moreover, only be recognized without ambiguity in faith as acts of God's sovereign power. They are above all signs of the coming kingdom of God. In them, God's kingdom is made proleptically present. The fact that the whole of mankind is brought to salvation and wholeness can be seen in these signs.

3.4 The Christological question

On the basis of his behaviour, message and actions, we are bound to return to our original question, asked at the end of our second section above: Who was this Jesus of Nazareth? It is not an easy question to answer. In the first place, we must accept that almost all the Christological titles – Son of God, Son of Man, Messiah, Prophet, servant of God and so on[13] – go back, not to the earthly Jesus, but to later proclamation in the early Church. Jesus did not proclaim himself. He proclaimed God and his kingdom. He did not teach any Christology, with the result that we can at the most only look for an indirect or implicit Christology of Jesus. Bultmann has already indicated the direction in which we should look, a way which has been followed by many subsequent theologians.[14] This way has led in fact to much more convincing results than the rather precise apolgetical approach in which an attempt is made to preserve individual sovereign titles as authentic words of Jesus himself.

It is also possible to take Jesus' behaviour as our

point of departure, since a certain Christology is undoubtedly implied in the unusual aspect of his behaviour and the sovereign freedom that is expressed in it. Unlike the prophets, who simply proclaimed the kingdom of God, Jesus also brought it. It began here and now in his miraculous actions: 'If it is by the finger of God that I cast out demons, then the kingdom of God has come upon you' (Lk 11:20). The connection between Jesus' person and his cause is made clear in this logion, which is generally accepted as authentic. Jesus in fact included his person in his cause. His activity, which is in this case the driving out of demons, and the coming of the kingdom of God were directly connected with each other. The kingdom of God already came in Jesus' activity and appearance. The same also applies to his proclamation, which we must now briefly consider.

In the contrasts presented in the Sermon on the Mount – the first, second and fourth are usually regarded as authentic – what is clearly expressed is: 'It was said to the men of old . . . but I say to you' (Mt 5:21, 27, 33). In other words, Jesus ventures to call the authority of Moses, the highest authority in Judaism, into question and to place himself above the word of God in the Old Testament. He claimed to be the messenger of the definitive Word of God. For this reason, no confirmation was needed for what he said and he used the word 'amen', which was generally employed to confirm what another person had said, to confirm his own pronouncement: 'Amen, amen, I say to you. . . .' An entire Christology is in fact implied in this linguistic usage that is so characteristic of Jesus.[15] He did not, in other words, do as the prophets had done in Israel and point from his word back to the Word of God: 'Thus says the Lord'. Jesus vouchsafed for his own word and spoke of his own authority, which was higher than that of the Old Testament. He was himself more than a prophet and we can only say that he himself speaks God's Word.

What was implicit and indirect in the sayings of the historical Jesus was made explicit and direct after the Easter event. The Christological titles of sovereignty and the whole Christology that followed the Easter event must be understood as the response made by the Christian community to Jesus' claim and his call to believers to come to a decision. These titles do not falsify Jesus' message in any way. On the contrary, they are fully in accordance with that message and make it more explicit. The unprecedented claim made by the earthly Jesus leads directly to the statement made in the fourth gospel: 'I and the Father are one' (Jn 10:30).

Even in the post-paschal levels of the New Testament, however, there are no really ontological statements that correspond to the later doctrine of the two natures of Christ. The Christology of the New Testament is rather functional, in other words, it contains statements that express Jesus' saving significance. It was less important for the New Testament authors to say who Jesus *was* than to say what he *meant* for us. If we were, however, to play one part of this statement off against the other, we would be seriously misunderstanding its significance, since it is very characteristic of Jesus that he completely identified himself with his function. He *was*, in other words, what he *meant*. His message and his person coincide and we are bound to say that his person is his function and that the two cannot be separated.[16]

Jesus saw his whole life as obedience to the Father and service of his fellow men. He wanted nothing for himself. From the standpoint of this obedience to God, he was entirely the man for others. He was committed

to this openness to God and to man and consumed by
this commitment until he died. In this way, he was, in
his person, the mode of existence of the rule of God's
love. He *was* so radical in this that he was, in his free
obedience as a man, the instrument for God's existence
and activity in human history. In this sense, he was
and *is* the Son of God. In his entirely human obedience
Jesus *is* God's mode of existence. This way we can say
that the later dogma of the Church, according to which
Jesus is fully man and fully God, is quite right. It is,
of course, historically conditioned, but it validly expresses, within the framework of that historically determined terminology, Jesus' cause,[17] even though it
now needs interpretation and can even be superseded.

Through this obedience, Jesus offers us a new possible human approach, because in his obedience to God
he was totally committed to his fellow men. In that
obedience, he also bore witness to a new mode of existence based on faith. Faith therefore means in the last
resort being admitted to Jesus' innermost attitude.
Jesus thus gives us the possibility of a new form of
freedom, a freedom that is expressed in service to our
fellow men. Within this outline of a new form of humanity everything that is great, noble and good in all
other human norms is included. On the other hand,
however, the Christian model of human behaviour is
also in many ways the opposite of other norms. We
can only learn how to live in faith in real life by
studying Jesus' own behaviour. He is, in a word, the
sign and the witness of faith.[18]

What is the situation with regard to this claim made
by Jesus? How can we know that he was right? It
would be meaningless to try to find proof of this claim,
but it can to some extent be verified. The inner truth
of the reality and the possibility of a new form of
humanity of the kind offered by Jesus can be estab-

lished by the fact that this truth is confirmed in the
phenomenon of human greatness and misery. Man
wavers betwen greatness and misery. Should he ack-
nowledge that the signs that encourage him to trust
in his greatness are right or should he follow those
that lead him to despair?
What is so convincing in Jesus' figure and message
is that both do full justice to greatness and misery.
Jesus points to man's greatness and reveals to him his
mission and his vocation. At the same time, however,
he also shows man his misery and that he is incapable
of conforming to this greatness, at least of his own
accord. In our knowledge of misery, we are preserved
from pride and, in our knowledge of greatness, we are
preserved from despair. Our true humanity is therefore revealed to us in Jesus Christ. This fact provides
a certain inner evidence of Jesus' claim and message.
Nowhere else can we find totally unambiguous statements, which do such full justice to the human situation, as we can in the life and message of Jesus Christ.
We are therefore bound to ask where else we should
and where else we might find such words of life.

Notes

    1. For the history of the quest for the historical Jesus, see A.
Schweitzer, *The Quest of the Historical Jesus* (London, 1954); W.
Kümmel, *The New Testament. The History of the Investigation of
its Problems* (New York, 1972; London, 1973); R. Slenczka, *Geschichtlichkeit und Personsein Jesu Christi. Studien zur christologischen Problematik der historischen Jesusfrage* (Göttingen, 1967).
    2. A. Schweitzer, *op. cit.*, p. 1 ff, 4.
    3. *Op. cit.*, p. 631
    4. *Dogmatic Constitution on Divine Revelation (Dei Verbum)*,
19.
    5. See H. Conzelmann, 'Zur Methode der Leben-Jesu-For-

schung', *Zeitschrift für katholische Theologie 56* (1959), Beiheft 1, 4.

6. R. Bultmann, 'Zur Frage der Christologie', *Glauben und Verstehen* I (Tübingen, 1933), p. 101. Of particular interest in this context is R. Bultmann, *Das Verhältnis der urchristlichen Christusbotschaft zum historischen Jesus* (Sitzungsbericht der Heidelberger Akademie der Wissenschaften) (Heidelberg, 1960).

7. E. Käsemann, 'Zum Problem des historischen Jesus', *Exegetische Versuche und Besinnungen* I (Göttingen, 1960), pp. 187–214; id., 'Sackgassen im Streit um den historischen Jesus', *op. cit.*, II (Göttingen, 1964), pp. 31–68. From the vast number of publications on this subject, the following are of special relevance: H. Ristow & K. Matthiae, eds., *Der historische Jesus und der kerygmatische Christus. Beiträge zum Christusverständnis in Forschung und Verkündigung* (Berlin, 1962); J. M. Robinson, *Kerygma und historischer Jesus* (Zürich & Stuttgart, 1960); J. R. Geiselmann, *Jesus der Christus* I: *Die Frage nach dem historischen Jesus* (Munich, 1965).

8. G. Bornkamm, *Jesus von Nazareth* (Stuttgart, 1956), pp. 18, 21 ff.

9. See M. Hengel, *War Jesus Revolutionär?* (Calwer Hefte 110) (Stuttgart, 1970).

10. E. Käsemann, *Der Ruf der Freiheit* (Tübingen, 1968), p. 52.

11. See R. Schnackenburg, *God's Rule and Kingdom* (London 1965). For what follows, see especially H. Schürmann, 'Das hermeneutische Hauptproblem der Verkündigung Jesu', *Gott in Welt (Festgabe für Karl Rahner)*, I (Freiburg, 1964), pp. 579–607.

12. See B. Thum, H. Haag, J. Schmid, A. Vögtle, A. Kolping & J. B. Metz, 'Wunder', *Lexikon für Theologie und Kirche*, X² (1965), pp. 1251–65; J. Gnilka & H. Fries, 'Zeichen/Wunder', *Handbuch Theologischer Grundbegriffe* II (1963), pp. 876–96; R. H. Fuller, *Interpreting the Miracles* (Philadelphia, 1963); F. Mussner, *Die Wunder Jesu. Eine Hinführung* (Munich, 1967); R. Pesch, *Jesu ureigene Taten? Ein Beitrag zur Wunderfrage (Quaetiones disputatae* 52 (Freiburg, 1970).

13. A. Vögtle, 'Jesus Christus', *Lexikon für Theologie und Kirche* V² (1960), pp. 922–32; H. Conzelmann, *Jesus* (Philadelphia, 1973); O. Cullmann, *Die Christologie des Neuen Testaments* (Tübingen, ²1958); F. Hahn, *Christologische Hoheitstitel. Ihre Geschichte im Frühen Christentum* (Göttingen, ²1964); J. Gnilka, *Jesus Christus nach den frühen Zeugnissen des Glaubens* (Munich, 1970).

14. R. Bultmann, *Theologie des Neuen Testaments* (Tübingen,

[2]1954), pp. 8, 44; id., *Das Verhältnis der urchristlichen Christusbotschaft zum historischen Jesus, op. cit.,* p. 16; H. Conzelmann,
op. cit; W. Marxsen, *Anfangsprobleme der Christologie* (Gütersloh,
1960), pp. 12, 16f, 35f, 38.
    15. H. Schlier, 'Amen', *Theologisches Wörterbuch zum Neuen
Testament* I (1933), p. 341: 'The whole of the Church's Christology
is contained in a nutshell in the *amen* that precedes Jesus' *lego
humin'*.
    16. K. Barth, *Kirchliche Dogmatik,* III/2 (Zürich, 1948),
pp. 66–9; W. Pannenberg, *Grundzüge der Christologie* (Gütersloh,
1964), pp. 345–61; H. Urs von Balthasar, 'Zwei Glaubensweisen',
Spiritus Creator (Einsiedeln, 1967), pp. 89f; J. Ratzinger, *Introduction to Christianity (London, 1969).* For the problem as a whole,
see H. Schlier, F. Mussner, F. Ricken & B. Welte, *Zur
Frühgeschichte der Christologie. Ihre biblische Anfänge und die
Lehrformel von Nikaia (Quaestiones disputatae* 51) (Freiburg,
1970).
    17. The term 'Jesus' cause' was first used by W. Marxsen in
connection with his interpretation of Jesus' resurrection (see note
3, chapter 4). Since then, it has become a popular theological
concept, frequently used without any meaningful content. It is,
however, a significant key-term in K. Schäfer's contribution,
'Rückfrage nach der Sache Jesu', to N. Greinacher, K. Lang & P.
Scheuermann, eds., *Im Sachen Synode* (Düsseldorf, 1970), pp. 150–
69. In this theological programme, however, the inseparable connection between Jesus' person and his cause, and between the
earthly Jesus and the risen Christ as well as the testimony borne
to the latter by the community of believers, is almost entirely
ignored. What has not been clearly recognized is that Jesus *is* his
cause in person, and that his cause can consequently only be
furthered because witness is borne to him in person as the living
Lord.
    18. For the connection between Jesus and faith, see G. Ebel-
ing, 'Jesus und Glaube', *Wort und Glaube* I, (Tübingen, 1960),
pp. 203–54; Hans Urs von Balthasar, 'Fides Christi', *Sponsa Verbi*
(Einsiedeln, 1960), pp. 45–79.

4 The truth of faith

4.1. Easter as the ground of faith

Nowadays, not for the first time in history, the believer has to ask again and again why he believes. As long as faith is not an unthinkingly accepted convention for him, he will also ask repeatedly how he can justify his faith intellectually and whether what he believes is true.

In the preceding chapters, I have offered only temporary answers to the question of the truth of faith. I have, for example, pointed to individual signs leading to faith and to Jesus of Nazareth as the sign and the witness of faith. I have not, however, answered this question completely. On the other hand, we have to recognize that, even in the case of Jesus himself, this question of the truth of faith was left open. After all, from the human point of view, he failed, since he was crucified. Like millions before him, he was defeated by the powers of violence and falsehood. Is the figure of Jesus of Nazareth, then, not a ground for believing, not in an ultimate meaning, but in the meaninglessness of life?

This is a difficult question. Jesus' cause was so closely identified with his person that, after his death, his disciples could not, even if they had wished to, have simply carried on by furthering his cause and

preserving it in their memory. When Jesus died in
person, his cause was dead and the truth of his message was fundamentally called into question. Paul was
therefore right to say: 'If Christ has not been raised,
your faith is futile. . . . If for this life only we have
hoped in Christ, we are of all men most to be pitied'
(1 Cor. 15: 17, 19). The answer that the early community of Christians gave to the question of their
truth of faith was therefore the message of God's raising Jesus from the dead. It was, the early Christians
believed, in this fact that God himself confessed his
faith in the earthly and crucified Jesus of Nazareth,
confirmed him and appointed him as Lord of the world.

This answer of the early Church is today, at least at
first sight, more problematical than helpful. It is true,
of course, that the well known rationalistic theories
– that Jesus only appeared to die and that it was an
illusion or a vision in the case of his resurrection –
now to a very great extent belong to the past, but the
fact remains that the resurrection is still a very difficult problem.[1]

Nowadays, the resurrection is not directly denied,
but it is subjected to a variety of interpretations. These
attempted interpretations seek to explain the resurrection of Jesus as a pure interpretament, in other
words, as a statement interpreting the matter that is
intended in a certain encoded form. Bultmann, for
example, regarded the resurrection as an interpretation of the saving significance of the cross.[2] Marxsen,
on the other hand, thought of it as an interpretation
of an event or experience of seeing, which gave rise to
various functions and brought about among the first
disciples the conviction that Jesus' cause was
continuing.[3]

All this sounds surprising, since the ground of our
faith and hope can never be the fact that Jesus lives

in the memory of his disciples, but only the fact that
he lives with God. The resurrection of Jesus, then, is
not an objective historical fact that can be objectively
and neutrally ascertained. The various interpretations
that are mentioned above are therefore right to the
extent that the word 'resurrection' is only an image,
taken from the waking of a sleeper and applied to a
completely different matter. Materially, then, this
waking or 'resurrection' did not, in the apocalyptic
terminology, mean a return to the old life, but the
beginning of a new life, the dawn of the new aeon. The
reality of this new life lies outside man's ordinary
experience. It is therefore not possible to speak about
it in any way other than that of the imagery of faith.

If we look at the question of the resurrection of Jesus
from the historical point of view, we need go back no
further than to the Easter testimonies of the first disciples, who claimed that they had seen the risen Lord
and had been sent by him (Lk 24:34; 1 Cor 15: 3–8,
Mt 28: 16–20; Gal 1: 11–16; 1 Cor 9:1). The resurrection itself is not described anywhere in any of the
canonical gospels (although it is, of course, in the
apocryphal gospels). Nothing is said either about the
way in which the risen Christ appeared. We should
not, however, imagine it to have been remarkably miraculous, since that would amount to doing away with
the faith of the first witnesses of the Easter event on
the basis of their revolutionary experience.

These first witnesses must therefore have seen in
faith and have been touched and directly involved by
Jesus Christ in such a way that he was given authority
in the faith of the disciples as the risen Lord.[4] It must
have been apparent to those disciples that the future
of God, which Jesus had promised to all men, also
applied to him in the first place, in other words, that
his person and his work had not, on the basis of God's

faithfulness, failed on the cross, but had a definitive future. The most important aspect of faith in the Easter event, then, is the ultimate revelation of who God is. He is the one whose power includes life and death and who 'calls into existence the things that do not exist' (Rom. 4:17). In the resurrection of Jesus, God ultimately defined himself and revealed his divinity. In him therefore it is possible to 'hope against hope' (Rom 4: 17f).

The ultimate ground of our faith, then, is the resurrection of Jesus and the kingdom of God that is definitively revealed in that resurrection. Jesus' being raised from the dead is the ground, beginning and appearance of a world that has ultimately been redeemed from the power of evil. It is, of course, true that the power of evil, lying, injustice and violence is still felt in our present dispensation, with the result that faith in the Easter event has from the very beginning always been called into question and has therefore also always been dependent on signs to establish its certainty. These critical questions and objectives are even to be found in the New Testament itself. Let us consider some of them and the response made by the New Testament authors briefly here.

The names of the original witnesses were recorded at a very early stage (1 Cor 15: 5–8) and references were made in Scripture to experiences at certain communal meals and, in many traditions at least, to the empty tomb. The latter was, however, never the most important element in the matter; it was only ever valid as a sign. It was with the help of this and other signs that attempts were made to give validity to faith in the Easter event, but it was understood at an early date that such signs are never open to only one interpretation – they can always be interpreted in many ways. It was possible, then, to explain the empty tomb as the result of an illusion (Mt 28. 13). In the same way, Paul also pointed to his own experiences in faith and the fact that, even in extreme affliction, he was always able to derive strength from that faith in the Easter event (2 Cor 1: 3–11). Again, he wanted it to be a sign and a manifestation of the risen Lord (2 Cor 4: 7–14). Asked for proof, he replied that believers should 'examine themselves to see whether they were holding to their faith (2 Cor 13:5). An experience giving validity to faith was only possible if the believer himself was involved or when the non-believer accepted faith and went through the experience of faith. Only then was it possible to experience the truth of that faith.[5] Only the man who let himself be drawn into the history that had begun with Christ could experience its truth. Only 'he who does what is true comes to the light' (Jn 3:21). The truth of faith can only be learnt in the life of faith.

In asking about the truth of faith, we should not take an understanding of truth that is alien to faith as our point of departure. We should rather take the scriptural understanding of truth[6] that is clear from the witness borne to the resurrection. Unlike other widespread concepts of truth, truth in the Bible is not simply a question of finding agreement between thought and reality (*adaequatio rei et intellectus*). Biblical truth is rather an event in which the original presupposition is proved valid. Truth cannot, in the biblical sense, be retained. It would be more correct to say that it presents itself and that it is directly connected with history. The full revelation of the truth of God will not be made until the end of time, when God will be everything to everyone (1 Cor 15:28). The truth of faith that we experience here and now is an anticipation in the form of a sign of this eschatological vision subject to the conditions of the present age. We may conclude therefore that faith is only possible in the light of hope.

4.2. The traditional ways of justifying faith

In the New Testament, these various ways of understanding the truth are not formulated in an elaborate theory for the justification of faith. It was not until the modern era, when conflict arose between faith on the one hand and a different understanding of truth based on what can be rationally verified that any attempt was made to develop a theory for the justification of faith. The most notable of these theories was that of the *analysis fidei* or the motive of faith.[7] This presented believers, however, with a serious dilemma. On the one hand, human responsibility for the act of faith had to be preserved, in the conviction that a blind act of faith was irresponsible and inhuman. It had therefore to be demonstrated that the act of faith could be made in an intellectually honest way. On the other hand, however, faith would no longer be faith if it had to be rationally proved. The question of the justification of faith was therefore the cross that tortured theologians.

The Church's teaching office condemned the two extremes – on the one hand, theological rationalism, converting faith into knowledge, and, on the other hand, fideism, in which faith was a blind leap into the dark and pure intuition.[8] In an attempt to find a way between these two extremes, a distinction was made in traditional apologetics between the real ground and motive of faith that can only be grasped in faith itself and the grounds of credibility that should make consent to faith humanly responsible.

The signs, such as miracles and prophecies, that

play a part in the New Testament as signs of faith are
usually accepted as grounds of credibility and, according to the traditional theory of the justification of faith,
their function is to show that there is more at work in
revelation than simply natural and human forces.

A somewhat different approach was followed in the
later apologetical movement known as the method of
immanence, the most important representative of
which was Maurice Blondel. In this method, these external grounds of credibility are replaced by inner mo-
tives that appeal less to man's intellect than to his
subjective readiness to accept faith. An attempt was
made to demonstrate how faith was in accordance with
man's subjective needs, mainly by pointing to his inner
beauty and the meaningful nature of his existence and
by showing that he is capable of providing an answer
to the social problems of his environment.

A third movement in apologetics was called the
method of providence. The important element in this
method was not the signs in the history of man's salvation, but the Church, as a 'great and perpetual motive of credibility and an irrevocable testimony of its
divine mission' by virtue of 'its admirable propagation,
its excellent holiness and inexhaustible fertility in all
that is good, its Catholic unity and invincible
stability'.[9]

All of these three methods have their own difficulties. At first sight, the third method would seem to
have the most insuperable difficulty of all, in that the
Church today is for many people an obstacle rather
than a help to faith. The second method, however, also
provides arguments for faith that are not immediately
convincing, since they are purely abstract until they
are put into practice and made credible in the community of believers. Christianity has, in other words,
to demonstrate in practice that it is in accordance with

the needs and demands of mankind. The first method, which places such emphasis on signs as grounds of credibility, also has its distinctive difficulty, which we must briefly discuss here.

As long ago as the eighteenth century, Lessing[10] pointed to a distinction that existed between miracles and prophecies that I myself experience and those that I know only as historical events that others are said to have experienced. Our certainty of salvation cannot be based on this kind of historical certainty, with the result that there is a need for 'proofs of the existence of the Spirit and his power'. Lessing therefore called for evidence of the credibility of faith in our present rather than our historical experience. What he meant by this is indicated at the end of his essay in his reference to the legendary words of the aging John in the apocryphal Testament of the Apostle John: 'Little children, love each other'. The credibility of faith has, in other words, to be demonstrated in love, which is the practice of faith. Love is the sign and the miracle *par excellence* which makes faith credible in the concrete.[11]

We may therefore summarize these three ways of proving the credibility of faith by criticizing them as follows. Faith cannot be made credible in a purely abstract and intellectual way. It has to be demonstrated in the community of believers. Its credibility is also dependent on that of the Church itself. It is not convincing to say in the abstract that faith is at the service of man's freedom while a system of fear from which freedom is absent operates in the Church and every movement towards freedom is regarded with deep suspicion and if possible suppressed. It is unacceptable to speak in exalted terms about the brotherhood of man while preserving a rule of absolute power. It is only possible to make the faith of the Church credible by setting about a serious renewal of the Church. The only really credible signs of faith are individual Christians and communities of Christians, who bear witness to the existence of faith by their lives.[12]

None of these ways of proving the credibility of faith are in fact proofs of faith itself. All that they can do is to establish the possibility, responsibility and meaningfulness of faith. They do not provide any evidence of what is believed. They are therefore no more than preambles of faith.[13] According to the traditional teaching of the Church, as defined in the first Vatican Council, the inner motive and the real ground of faith can only be provided by the authority of the God who reveals himself (*auctoritas Dei revelantis*). This authority cannot err, not can it lead others into error.[14] The ultimate ground of certainty on which faith is based, then, is the truth and the truthfulness of God himself.

Two aspects of this definition in the Dogmatic Constition *Dei Filius* of Vatican I are worth noting here. The first is that the Constitution speaks not of *auctoritas Dei imperantis*, but of *auctoritas Dei revelantis*. It is not, in other words, a question of pure authority as such. We are not told that God has revealed something and that is that. This kind of positivism with regard to faith and this kind of obedience are not in accordance with the teaching of the Church. The certainty of faith is rather based in the evidence and authority of the truth of God. This means that problems of faith cannot be reduced – as they often are nowadays – to problems of obedience. We do not, then, believe the Church. We believe because we are convinced of the truth of the God who reveals himself.

The second aspect of the definition is that the ground of faith is neither miracles and prophecies nor the

Church and its official pronouncements. The ground and motive of faith is the truth of God alone. Faith does not imply a need to regard miraculous actions or pronouncements about faith that are claimed to be authoritative as true. On the contrary, it implies a readiness to assent to God as the ground and the objective of man's existence. The believer does not believe in the Church or its dogmas – he believes in God. This fundamental datum cannot be adequately included within any of the Church's dogmas. God's truth is greater than any statement that we can make about it. This means that we can and must make a distinction between the ground of faith and man's ideas of and pronouncements about faith, which are always historically conditioned.

Since God, as the real ground of faith, is ultimately inaccessible to human knowledge, man can only know him in faith and recognize him as the ultimate authority if this makes itself known. Every time man attempts to seize hold of God by his own efforts, then, he will inevitably fail to grasp him and every time he attempts to know him by his own efforts, he will misunderstand him. He will try to understand him in accordance with the conditioned nature of his own ability to know, make him finite and end by degrading him to the level of an idol. It must therefore be God's task to make it possible for us to know him. It is also God's task to give man the conditions governing man's knowledge of him. It is only in this way that God can continue to be the Lord of his Word and that his divinity can become the ground of our certainty of faith.

This is what the scholastic theologians meant by their theory of the light of faith and the illuminating grace of faith. This theory does not represent an objective content of faith. It is rather the condition provided by God himself which makes faith possible. It has as its object a corresponding connaturality and congeniality of human knowledge. The grace of faith is therefore not a stop-gap for a defective understanding. On the contrary, it provides a new and clearer way of seeing and enables us to understand the signs of faith more precisely. We can, in this context, speak with P. Rousselot of the 'eyes of faith'.[15] The Holy Spirit plays an important part in this process as the power which makes the kingdom of God, which dawned with the first Easter, present. The same Spirit also involves us in the new beginning of life of faith and in him we are able to anticipate here and now the signs of the coming kingdom.

4.3. Giving an account of faith today

In the preceding sections of this chapter, I have outlined the most important aspects of a theological justification of faith. This outline is, however, ultimately not entirely satisfactory, because our problems today begin precisely where the theological exposition ceases. It might well have been enough, at a time when God and his authority were presuppositions that were accepted unquestioningly by everyone in society, to refer to God as the ultimate ground and motive of faith. Living as we do since the Enlightenment, however, a reference to an absolute truth calling for unconditional obedience would be regarded as a sign to end the dialogue and an expression of authoritarian thinking. There can be no doubt that most representatives of critical rationalism such as K. Popper, H. Albert and W. Bartley would regard any theology or philosophy that is in search of an ultimate ground of certainty as an attempt to break off dialogue and to seek refuge in commitment. They would also see in it a dangerous claim to infallibility and obedience and an equally dangerous tendency towards the persecution of and a discrimination against those who thought differently. Rationalists would oppose this type of thinking based on infallibility with the principle of fallibility, rejecting dogmatic and absolute principles in favour of purely hypothetical, provisional and limited ones which could then be subjected to critical testing and verification. Over and against such a closed and monolithic way of thinking, they would uphold a fundamentally open and pluralistic philosophy.

We should not be under any illusion about this — the way of thinking briefly described in the preceding paragraph as opposing any search for an ultimate ground of faith is extremely widespread today. Modern man is tired of the philosophical and theological quest for eternal truth and prefers to limit himself to concrete questions that can be answered rationally. The rejection of the quest for an ultimate ground and motive can also be found, for example, in the later philosophical writings of Martin Heidegger and the negative dialectics of Theodor Adorno.

What we have here is clearly a new direction in philosophy. This new way of thinking does not, however, need to be in advance and in every respect opposed to theology. One of the main reasons for this is that it contains certain leading ideas which have always been present in any negative theology and philosophy and especially in mystical theology, a tradition in which the unattainable and withdrawn nature of the absolute faith has always been recognized. Thomas Aquinas, for example, taught, in the tradition of the negative theology, that we know what God is not rather than what he is.[16] If we are convinced that God is hidden, we cannot regard him as the calculable ground and guarantee of our theological and church system. Anyone who believes in God as the one who is always greater must always be open to new experiences and new knowledge.

Unfortunately, this profound insight became lost in the course of time. We have come to know much too much about God in theology, especially in the more recent theories of the justification of faith. In the way in which they pose and answer the question concerning the ultimate ground of certainty of faith, they are extremely dependent on modern post-Cartesian philosophy, in which the question of an ultimate ground of knowledge has often been raised. In both cases, very similar attempts have been made to understand reality from one vantage point.

This way of thinking, however, is hardly in accordance with the biblical understanding of truth. As I have already pointed out, Scripture does not refer back to an ultimate ground – it points forward to the future anticipated by Jesus' resurrection. Our certainty of faith is our certainty of hope. This means that faith will always be contentious in history and that the believer will never have his faith behind him – it will always be ahead of him. He is bound to repeat the words: 'Lord, I believe; help my unbelief!' (Mk 9:23). There is not only a possible *simul iustus et peccator*, but also a *simul fidelis et infidelis*.[17] The believer's faith is always at risk. Faith is not closed; it is always an open system.

What has to be done, then, is to think out the traditional doctrine of the certainty of faith and doubt about faith anew and, in this process, to resist the old clerical temptation to form an integralist synthesis in a monolithic understanding of truth. Precisely because faith is essentially an eschatological faith in hope, it has to be exposed again and again to criticism and verification. We have to try again and again to show, in discussion with those who think differently from ourselves, that faith points to the future and that it can make that future known to man.

Faith is always on the way and is always looking for signs. Those who believe are not in the position of those blessed who are already in possession or of those who dispense criticism in a spirit of self-satisfaction. They must be at one with those who are seeking and asking and an inspiration to them. Faith must not be a refuge for those who already believe and are anxious for security. It must rather be a focal point for holy restlessness.

Despite this, however, theologians are bound to be opposed to the method of trial and error especially if this method is accepted as an ultimate position. Is this position really as open as it claims to be or does it not enclose man with dogmatic intolerance in his own finiteness? Does it in this way do full justice to man's search for meaning and to the claims made by his freedom and thinking? Or does it not rather set up no-entry signs at those points where man wants and has to go on seeking? Is it not, after all, man's nature to pursue the whole reality? Is it not also true to say that an ultimate commitment does not lead to a loss of freedom? Surely it leads to freedom, since it prevents us from losing our freedom by becoming the victims of every passing moment. Do we not encounter, in the freedom of our fellow man, an unconditional claim that cannot and should not be exposed to experimentation? And can man's infinite freedom ever be an ultimate position if freedom is not present in the depths of reality? Is it therefore a contradiction to speak of an absolute authority of freedom and is this not a description of what we mean when we speak of God and his rule?

This clearly brings us to the centre of the present controversy and to the point where we encounter the real ground of faith, the point where ultimate decisions have to be made. The question that arises at this point is: Are truth, meaning and freedom only devised and made by man or are they established in advance so that man may decide? Is it possible, in other words, to say that absolute freedom (or absolute meaning) *is* or ought we rather to say that this freedom (or this meaning) only *becomes* by being established by man? Are ontological statements, then, permitted within the framework of historical thinking or are they demanded? Are we able and obliged to say, in faith, that God *is* as the absolute future of man and that the certainty of our hope can only be justified within what Ernst Bloch has called this 'future with the dispensation of being'?

What is involved in this fundamental question is the essential decision of faith. It is not possible to find proofs for this fundamental act, only references. All the signs that I have mentioned can be references to the fact that meaning is established in advance, that is, before man's models of meaning. The first disciples' experiences of Easter were, for example, a reference for them that a new beginning was established in a completely irreducible way, that meaning had been victorious over meaninglessness and that love was stronger than death (Heb. 8:6).

Our own experience is also a reference for us. How, for example, could we ask about meaning at all if we had not already experienced it in our lives? It is, however, only when man tries to live by thankfully receiving this previously existing meaning that he can escape from the merciless pressure of achievement and production that characterizes contemporary society. 'Meaning is grace. This statement contains an implied

criticism of our contemporary society and its emphasis
on meaning based on man's achievement and utility'.[18]
It is only when man's purpose is firmly rooted in
what is ultimately without purpose that he can escape
from the contemporary emphasis on meaning as purpose. The truth of faith – God's divinity – is demonstrated in the fact that faith makes it possible for man
to be human. The claim of God's rule and kingdom is
at the same time addressed to man. Faith is something
that is expected and demanded of man. It is the task
of the Church as a whole and of each individual Christian to make this credible in the concrete.

Notes

1. See K. H. Rengstorf, *Die Auferstehung Jesu*, (Witten,
[4]1960); H. Grass, *Ostergeschehen und Osterberichte* (Göttingen,
[3]1964); J. Kremer, *Das älteste Zeugnis von der Auferstehung Christi. Eine bibeltheologische Studie zur Aussage und Bedeutung von
1 Kor 15, 1–11* (Stuttgarter Bibelstudien 17) (Stuttgart, [2]1967); P.
Seidensticker, *Die Auferstehung Jesus in der Botschaft der Evan-
gelisten. Ein traditionsgeschichtlicher Versuch zum Problem der
Sicherung der Osterbotschaft in der apostolischen Zeit* (Stuttgarter
Bibelstudien 26) (Stuttgart, 1967); W. Marxsen, U. Wilckens, G.
Delling & H.-G. Geyer, *Die Bedeutung der Auferstehungsbotschaft
für den Glauben an Jesus Christus* (Gütersloh, 1967); K. Lehmann,
*Auferweckt am dritten Tag nach der Schrift. Früheste Christologie,
Bekenntnisbildung und Schriftauslegung im Lichte von 1 Kor 15,
3–5* (Quaestiones disputatae 38) (Freiburg, 1968); H. Schlier, *Über
die Auferstehung Jesus Christi* (Einsiedeln, 1968); F. Mussner, *Die
Auferstehung Jesu* (Munich, 1969); G. Kegel, *Auferstehung Jesu
– Auferstehung der Toten. Eine traditionsgeschichtliche Untersuchung zum Neuen Testament* (Gütersloh, 1970); H. Ludochowski,
*Auferstehung – Mythos oder Vollendung des Lebens? (Der Christ
in der Welt* V/13) (Asschaffenburg, 1970).
2. R. Bultmann, 'Neues Testament und Mythologie. Das Problem der Entmythologisierung der neutestamentlichen
Verkündigung', *Kerygma und Mythos* I (Hamburg, [4]1960), pp. 44–
8; *id., Das Verhältnis der urchristlichen Christusbotschaft zum*

historischen Jesus (Sitzungsberichte der Heidelberger Akademie der Wissenschaften) (Heidelberg, 1960), pp. 26f; the ambiguous statement 'the meaning of faith in the Easter event is to believe in the Christ who is present in the kerygma' can be found on p. 27. See, however, the interpretation provided by G. Hasenhüttl, *Der Glaubensvollzug. Eine Begegnung mit R. Bultmann aus katholischem Glaubensverständnis* (Koinonia 1) (Essen, 1963), pp. 91–5.

3. W. Marxsen, *Die Auferstehung Jesu als historisches und als theologisches Problem* (Gütersloh, 1964); id, *Die Auferstehung Jesu von Nazareth* (Gütersloh, 1968).

4. See G. Ebeling, *Das Wesen des christlichen Glaubens* (Tübingen, 1959), pp. 80–3.

5. Hans Urs von Balthasar, *Herrlichkeit. Eine theologische Ästhetik* I (Einsiedeln, 1961), pp. 217–20. See also E. Güttgemanns, *Der leidende Apostel und sein Herr. Studien zur paulinischen Christologie* (Forschung zur Religion und Literatur der Alten und Neuen Testament) (Göttingen, 1963).

6. See A. Schlatter, *Der Glaube im Neuen Testament* (Tübingen,⁵1963), pp. 551–61; H. von Soden, 'Was ist Wahrheit?', *Urchristentum und Geschichte* I (Tübingen, 1951), pp. 1–24; G. Quell, G. Kittel & R. Bultmann, *'aletheia', Theologisches Wörterbuch zum Neuen Testament* I (1933), pp. 223–48; W. Kasper, *Dogma unter dem Wort Gottes* (Mainz, 1965), pp. 65–84.

7. See the survey of this doctrine and the full bibliography provided by F. Malmberg, *'Analysis fidei', Lexikon für Theologie und Kirche* I² (1957), pp. 477–83; H. Fries, 'Glaubensmotive', *Lexikon für Theologie und Kirche* IV² (1960), pp. 943–5; and the articles by J. Alfaro and K. Palmer on faith in *Sacramentum Mundi* (London & New York, 1969).

8. Denzinger-Schönmetzer, 3008–3014, 3031–3036 = new series 35–41, 53–58. See also J. H. Pottmeyer, *Der Glaube vor dem Anspruch der Wissenschaft. Die Konstitution über den katholischen Glauben 'Dei Filius' des 1. Vatikanischen Konzils und die unveröffentlichten theologischen Voten der vorbereitenden Kommission* (Freiburger Theologische Studien 87) (Freiburg, 1968).

9. Denzinger–Schönmetzer 3013 = new series 356.

10. G. E. Lessing, 'Über den Beweis des Geistes und der Kraft (1777)', *Gesammelte Werke* VIII (Berlin, 1956), pp. 9–16.

11. See Hans Urs von Balthasar, *Glaubhaft ist nur Liebe* (Einsiedeln, 1963).

12. This connection was rightly emphasized by H. Küng in *The Church* (London, 1967).

13. See G. Muschalek, 'Praeambula fidei', *Lexikon für Theologie und Kirche* VIII² (1963), pp. 653–7.

14. Denzinger-Schönmetzer 3008 = new series 35.

15. P. Rousselot, *Die Augen des Glaubens* (Einsiedeln, 1963). See also E. Kunz, *Glaube-Gnade-Geschichte. Die Glaubenstheologie des Pierre Rousselot* (Frankfurt am Main, 1969).

16. Thomas Aquinas, *Summa Theologiae* I, q. 2, *prooemium*; see also Denzinger-Schönmetzer, 806 = new series 156.

17. J. B. Metz in *Concilium* 1 (1965).

18. H. Gollwitzer, *Krummes Holz – aufrechter Gang. Zur Frage nach dem Sinn des Lebens* (Munich, 1970), p. 46.

5 The act of faith

5.1 Faith as a universal phenomenon

So far, I have discussed the situation and the place of faith, its signs, the witness borne to faith and the truth of faith. I may almost have given the impression that faith was a hypostasis existing in and for itself. In fact, however, faith only exists as an action performed by a man who believes. It only exists when a person commits himself to the truth of the proclamation of the kingdom of God, and it is only when this occurs that the kingdom of God is present in the concrete in history. The truth of faith can only be experienced in this personal commitment, in other words, in the act of faith. What, then, is this act of faith? What is believing? How is it done?

The word 'believe' – and even more so the whole phenomenon to which this word points – has many different meanings and has always been the object of controversy. The earlier problems still continue to make themselves felt now, so that it is still valuable to consider these traditional controversies today. Let us briefly survey these and their contemporary counterparts here. In the controversy between the Franciscan theologians working within the Augustinian tradition and the Dominican, Thomist theologians, the question was whether faith was primarily an act of

love or an act of the will or the intellect. Quite an
important part is also played in the contemporary debate about faith by the traditional problem of fiducial
or confessing faith. In this problem, the question that
arises is whether faith is basically a trust in God's
mercy and forgiveness of sins or whether it contains
an element of confession. This was the traditional controversy between the Reformers and Catholic theologians. In present-day theological language, the
question takes a different form, namely: Is faith synonymous with keeping to revealed truths and with
regarding dogmatically defined traditions as true, or
is it being existentially concerned and committed?

H. Halbfas insisted that faith was not an object, but
a manner or way of understanding reality,[2] whereas,
at very much the same time, Dorothee Sölle was sug-
gesting that it was a particular way of being present
and was primarily determined by practice.[3] These different interpretations of the concept of believing make
it difficult to reach agreement in the present crisis of
faith. What is for some a loss and even a destruction
is for others a liberation of faith from its imprisonment
in dogmatism. Different languages are spoken on
each side of the frontier, a frontier which nowadays
does not separate the different religious confessions,
but runs through them.

Before trying to deal with this problem, it would be
valuable to discuss the meaning of the word 'believe',
since a clarification of the concept should help to clar-
ify the matter itself. Let us first of all consider the
everyday meaning of the word. We say, for example:
'I believe that Mr Jones has gone away'. When we say
something like this, what we mean is that we have
reasons for making such an assertion, but that these
reasons are not sufficient for us to make a firm statement. In this case, then, believing is a defective form

of knowing. It is certain enough to be superior to a
mere opinion, which is something that takes the truth
of the opposite into account, but it is inferior to knowledge, which can rely on sufficient reasons.

This everyday concept of belief has to some extent
determined the theological tradition, in which faith
has often been defined as *cum assensione cogitare*. In
this definition, the rational reasons that are lacking
are supplemented by the command of the will to consent. Faith is seen as an intellectual achievement, a
sacrificium intellectus and, in its extreme form, a de-
cisionistic keeping to a special ideological content.
What we find underlying this understanding of faith
is a clearly defined ideal of knowledge – Descartes'
idea clara et distincta. In this, exact knowledge that
can be ascertained and verified occupies the most important place.

Another everyday usage of the word 'believe' will
show, however, how little we can take this understanding of faith and its underlying epistemology and anthropology for granted. If we reply to a promise or an
assurance made by someone else with the words: 'Yes,
I believe you', we do not mean: 'You cannot give me
sufficient proof of your honesty, but I have sufficient
objective reasons for thinking that the situation is as
you say it is'. We also do not say: 'I believe those
reasons', but 'I believe you'. Belief here is not related
to objective reasons, but to a person. It is a personal
act of trust and establishes a mutual bond between
persons. As a personal act, it includes the will and the
intellect in their original unity in the human person.
It is, in other words, an act performed by the whole
person.

Attempts have in recent years been made to provide
a better and deeper foundation for Christian faith on
the basis of this personal understanding of faith. It is

possible to show that no one can live simply on knowledge that can be objectively proved and that decisions
cannot be made simply on the basis of that knowledge,
at least in the most critical situations in life. Human
life is rather based on trust and faith. It is not possible
for men to live together without this mutual trust.
Nonetheless, it is also not possible for anyone to prove
to another person that he can be trusted in the real
sense of the word.

We may therefore conclude that faith is not a defective way of knowing. It is, on the contrary, a basic
human act in its own right. The comparison, however,
only helps us a little in our attempt to justify Christian
faith. Personal trust can only be valid for the one who
is concerned in the transaction. This is especially clear
in the love relationship between two people which is
often quoted as a parallel in this case. Like faith, love
cannot be verified or proved, but it does establish an
exclusive relationship between two people which has
a certain 'evidence' for those two alone. Faith, on the
other hand, makes a universal claim and is missionary. For this reason, the personal aspect of dialogue is
not sufficient as a justification of faith. It even provides
the basis for a privatistic misunderstanding of faith,
by confining it to the purely private sphere and obscuring its public aspect. One almost has the impression that there is a tendency here towards a closed
sectarian attitude and a reluctance to give an account
to all men for the hope contained in faith (1 Pet 3:15).

If, then, we are to have a better understanding of
Christian faith, a third aspect must be considered.
This third aspect is not expressed in our everyday
usage of the word 'believe', but the matter of faith is
quite certainly involved in it. It can perhaps best be
outlined in the following way. In certain critical situations in my life, the question arises spontaneously: Is

my life as a whole successful and meaningful or is it
a meaningless failure? I am not thinking here exclusively of my own life as such. I am also concerned with
whether or not the whole of reality has any meaning
for me. It is quite possible for personal disappoint-
ments to lead to metaphysical crises. In asking about
the meaning of life, then, I am at the same time concerned with the meaning of the whole of reality.

In theory, this question can be rejected as inadmis-
sible. In practice, however, none of us can escape from
it. Life and its decisions cannot be set aside. Each one
of us lives according to some model of existence. In
practice, then, each of us has at one time or another
already found some answer to this question. It cannot,
however, be answered in the same way as individual
questions, because the whole of reality cannot be
grasped in the same way as individual realities. Reality as a whole embraces all the different individual
questions. For this reason, it cannot be satisfactorily
objectivized. A further reason why it cannot be objectivized is because we are ourselves included within
that total reality. We are involved in every answer
that we give: *mea res agitur.*

Certain questions, then, are of fundamental importance. They are concerned with life itself and whether
it is meaningful or meaningless. They may be about
hope or despair. They certainly have to do with the
ultimate direction in which our existence is moving.
In such cases, purely factual knowledge is not involved. Each one of us believes in his own way. Even
the unbeliever – the person who does not believe in
the Christian sense of the word – believes in his own
way in cases such as this. Even his lack of faith is a
fundamental decision which can, like the decision of
faith, appeal to individual traces that cannot, like
faith itself, be proved or verified.

I may, therefore, summarize what I have said in this section in the following way. Faith is a fundamental act made by man. The question of faith arises not only in personal encounter, but also wherever the whole human reality is involved. Faith, then, is the fundamental act on which the whole of our human existence is based and within which the meaning of the whole of reality is revealed to us.

5.2 The biblical understanding of faith

So far, I have confined myself to very formal statements. My results have shown that every person who does not want his life to result in failure is bound to make a decision regarding faith and direct his life towards ultimate values. I have not, however, discussed the nature of this ultimate meaning. It is not in any sense necessary to provide a specifically Christian answer to this question about the meaning of the total reality. This meaning can, after all, be interpreted in many different ways – atheistically, pantheistically, naturalistically and materialistically, nihilistically or theistically, in a Christian or in a non-Christian sense. A possible way of understanding the world and the whole of the human reality is provided by all the great religious, intellectual, literary and political traditions of mankind. As a result, no one begins with no presuppositions at all when he comes to question the meaning of his own existence. He has also to come to terms with all these historical traditions in his search for his own identity and that of the world and ask whether they do justice to the reality of human life and if so how they contribute to the human situation.

Here, I shall, of course, confine myself to the Christian interpretation of the meaning of reality as a whole and ask: What is the Christian offer? What is the specifically Christian way in which man can find himself and his world? What, in other words, is the Christian answer to the question of human happiness?

The first thing that strikes us in the Old Testament[4] is that there is no technical term for our concept 'believe'. The two related words *pistis*, faith, and *pisteuein*, to believe, used in the Septuagint, the Greek translation of the Old Testament, translate a number of different words and concepts in the Hebrew text. Of these, however, there is one basic word in Hebrew that is particularly in accordance with the idea of faith and that is the verb *'āman*, a form of which has been used throughout the history of the Christian liturgy as an affirmation: Amen.

This word is in the first place a formal concept, meaning that a matter is form, reliable and certain and that it keeps to what it promises. In the case of faith, then, it implies that man's existence is certain on the basis of trust in a previously existing faithfulness and firmness. According to the Old Testament, man can only have firm ground under his feet if he relies entirely on God. Whereas it is not possible to rely on man – *omnis homo mendax* – Yahweh is faithfulness in person. He has, through his convenant with man, made it possible for man to have security and certainty in life. According to the Old Testament authors believing is saying amen to God and basing one's whole existence on Yahweh. Man can find security and a safe refuge only with Yahweh, who is the sole reliable foundation not only for the life of the individual, but for that of the whole people. The classical text in which we find this understanding of Old Testament faith is Is 7.9: 'If you do not make your existence firm [believe] in Yahweh, you will not have a firm existence'.

Turning to the New Testament, we find the concept 'believe' used in the synoptic gospels surprisingly for the most part in reports of miraculous healings. The concept of faith used in this context, then, has no deep theological content. It simply points to man's helplessness and his trust in the power of God active in Jesus. The believer is convinced that, even though help and healing cannot come from man, everything is possible with God (see, for example, Mk 10: 27 par). In the same way, 'all things are possible to him who believes' (Mk 9: 23). Faith, then, is a sharing in God's power. The believer enables God to act by entrusting nothing to himself and everything to God.[5] Faith is a vacuum to be filled by God and in this way a participation in the power of God. Man is therefore made whole in faith: 'Your faith has made you well' (Mk 10: 52). Faith in the New Testament sense, then, is man's salvation and certainty.

In the later levels of the New Testament, however, this all-embracing understanding of faith seems to have been lost. Martin Buber pointed out that two different ways of understanding faith are present in the Bible.[6] These two ways, which are represented by the Old Testament and Paul, are irreconcilable in Buber's opinion. He tried to show that the Old Testament understanding of faith as the achievement of a state of trust in God was reduced by Paul to a dogmatic faith that was confessed by the believer. The 'I believe that' of the Old Testament became, Buber maintained, faith as an object in Paul.

There can be no doubt that the content of faith was of fundamental importance for Paul. Faith for him was always faith in Jesus Christ and, as such, it was inseparably linked to those who were sent with the task of bearing witness to it — 'Faith comes from what is heard' (Rom 10: 17). Paul's concentration of faith on Christ is connected with the fundamental change that had taken place, with the crucifixion and resurrection of Jesus, in the history of salvation. The New Testament is not simply an extension of the Old — it is really a *New* Testament. This is why there is, in it, a break in the understanding of faith.

We should not, however, play these two ways of understanding faith off against each other. Even in the Old Testament, faith, which is primarily understood as trust, is also a response to God's faithfulness as experienced in history. As a result, there are also confessions of faith in the Old Testament. Faith is also present in the New Testament as trust. It is encountered in the synoptic gospels as a faith aroused by Jesus himself. In such cases, it is connected to the coming of Jesus and implies a Christological confession. The formula: 'Amen, amen, I say to you' is very characteristic of Jesus' way of speaking. It is, however, a very unusual way of speaking, which points to a total certainty on Jesus' part and to the fact that he regarded God himself as vouchsafing for his words and even that the truth and reality of his words were the truth and reality of God himself.

This 'amen', then, contains an entire Christology in a nutshell. Jesus Christ is 'the Amen, the faithful and true witness' of faith (Rev. 3.14) who arouses the amen of faith in others. There is a clear connection here with Paul's theology of faith. When he speaks of faith in Jesus Christ, he is speaking not only of a faith that is directed towards Christ, but also of a faith that implies a being admitted into Jesus' innermost attitude towards the Father. In its Christological roots, the New Testament understanding of faith is not in any sense below the level of the understanding of faith in the

Old Testament. Faith is understood in a more radical
way in the New Testament which transcends the Old
Testament understanding. In the New Testament, believing also means saying 'amen' to God with all the
consequences that that consent implies. Jesus is not
only the believer *par excellence*. He is also the one who
sets us free and thus arouses us to faith. Imitating
Jesus is therefore not only an external imitation. It is
also an imitation in faith.

I may summarize what I have said here in the following way. Faith is a fundamental decision on the
part of man in which he finds himself, his own way of
life, others and the whole of reality by finding God. In
faith, man hands himself over to God and says 'amen'
to God. He bases his whole existence on God without
reservation when he believes.

Faith is not simply an intellectual act or an act of
the will. It includes the whole man and every aspect
of the human reality. It does not apply exclusively to
the private and purely personal sphere of man's life.
It also has an equally important public and even political aspect. This is why faith is not simply a Christian act of the same kind as other acts. It is not simply
parallel with hope and love. It embraces the whole of
Christian existence, including hope and love, which
can be seen as two ways in which faith is realized. In
the imitation of Jesus, being a Christian means being
a believer. Being a Christian is defined by faith and
by faith alone.

If we understand the word 'believe' in this all-embracing sense, it should be possible to have a Catholic
sola fide. (In its condemnation of the doctrine of *sola
fide*, the Council of Trent presupposed a much narrow-
er concept of faith.) We can therefore say that the idea
of a holy person, which is so remote from our contemporary way of thinking, really means nothing other

than a completely believing person and, if we want to know what believing means, we must learn from the great saints of the Church.

5.3. Prayer as the emergency of faith

It would take me too far away from my central theme to discuss in detail here all the aspects of this all-embracing understanding of faith. I shall be dealing later with various individual aspects such as the part played by hope, political and social factors involved in faith and the element of confession. At present, however, I would prefer to limit myself to one way in which faith is expressed, since this is an aspect that has played quite an important part in recent debate about faith and is of fateful significance. I refer, of course, to the articulation of faith in prayer.[7]

Prayer is the emergency of faith. In prayer, the essential element of the act of faith is expressed in the most concrete way possible. Even more significantly, however, all the problems of the present crisis in faith are concentrated in the focal point of prayer. All attempts at a re-interpretation of Christian faith come together to a greater or lesser degree at this point of prayer. In prayer, then, we say 'to be or not to be' with regard to faith.

An objection that is often raised to the traditional understanding of faith in prayer is that it presupposes that man in prayer has an understanding of his existence that is completely different from that of the rest of his life. In the rest of our lives, it is thought, we deal with our problems ourselves. In prayer, on the other hand, it is presupposed that we address God as the one who is over and against us and count on his direct intervention in the course of world history. Marginal situations are reserved for prayer – in normal situations we behave differently.

In literature, this criticism of prayer was most impressively expressed by Bertolt Brecht in his play *Mother Courage*. When the enemy troops come close to the unprotected city of Halle, the peasant family knows that nothing more can be done but pray. The dumb girl Kattrin, however, seizes a drum and uses it to warn the sleeping citizens. She is shot, but the others escape alive. Dorothee Sölle made this comment about this scene in the play: 'Kattrin's drumming gives prominence to the age-old misuse of prayer. Save yourself and pray for others. Words addressed to a higher power instead of actions performed for those near to us. Kattrin's drumming shows that pious, subjectively authentic prayer is the alibi of those who do not commit themselves.[8]

This criticism, however, points rather to a very widespread misunderstanding and an equally widespread misuse of prayer – a misuse that is as common as the real concern of prayer. To use prayer as an alibi for action is not simply a misuse – it is also a perversion and a confusion of prayer with superstition. Dorothee Sölle was also aware of this and consequently tried to re-interpret prayer in a more subtle way, instead of criticizing it crudely. In her opinion, prayer should not be reserved for extreme emergencies and used only in marginal situations. The real place of prayer was for her the 'native country of life' and it was not an activity limited by space, time and object, but a reality embracing all other spheres of existence, including waking and sleeping, work and leisure and production and consumption.

Another argument in the same direction of a secular, non-religious understanding of prayer was put foward by the Anglican theologian J. A. T. Robinson some years ago in a book which was apparently popular, but which was in fact not at all easy to read: *Honest to God*. In this book, Robinson suggested that God was the profundity of our human intersubjective experience and that prayer was therefore not a series of particular human acts in which man turned away from the world and towards God. Man, he maintained, found God only in the world and above all in his fellow men. He believed that praying for another person meant exposing oneself and him to the common ground of man's being. It meant, in other words, seeing one's interest in the other person in the light of what concerned both parties unconditionally, that is, admitting God to the relationship. Any other form of prayer, Robinson insisted, was simply a form of initiation or practice or else inner recollection in depth.[9] It is clear, then, that the object of this kind of prayer is not God as the transcendent person, but the world or the other human being. God is, as it were, the medium or the absolute depths in which I am absolutely and unconditionally concerned with that other human being. Prayer in this sense means therefore knowing the other in God and knowing God in the other and experiencing daily life in its depths.

   This clearly brings us to the critical point and indeed to the nerve-centre of our contemporary understanding of faith. It would hardly be possible to argue with Robinson unless we were ready to take his quite legitimate concern seriously. It is certainly not possible for Christians to regard an act of faith or a prayer as a spiritual movement up to God that at the same time ignores the world and one's fellow men. An act of faith conceived in this way would not treat God as the absolute reality, but rather as a partial entity and even as a finite idol. This idea of a God who fills in the gaps is contrary to the mutual relationship between the love of God and the love of one's fellow men, a relationship which forms a constitutive element in the attitude and the teaching of Jesus of Nazareth.

However much we may object to the practice of filling in the gaps in human knowledge and activity with God and prayer – and it is right to object to this – we cannot deny that these gaps exist. I am not referring here to partial or categorical gaps that can be overcome, but to gaps of the kind that accompany man's finite existence and characterize humanity as such. This 'gap' or limitation that is given with man's being itself, his finiteness, is the place where faith – and together with faith, prayer – are the most meaningful and the most direct expression of his fundamental situation. It is only possible, however, to recognize this limitation that is given with man's being as such and at the same time not to despair about it if we are, as human beings, borne up and embraced by a freedom which sets our human freedom free for itself. This basic situation, in which man's freedom appeals to God's freedom and only God's freedom can make human freedom possible, is expressed most clearly in prayer. Man's fundamental relationship with God is articulated in prayer, which is the expression of his indebted existence. Prayer is also the act *par excellence* in which man hands himself over to God in order to receive himself from God in a new way.

This brings me to one of the oldest and most fundamental definitions of prayer – the raising of man to God. This process of raising up, however, takes place through the world and not past it. Since, however, it articulates the limitation that is given with man's humanity and the world and declares itself, despite its commitment, to be ultimately helpless and powerless, it is independent of activity in the world. In this independence, prayer is not a phenomenon existing alongside life as a whole. It is rather the truth that transcends life and the world. The difference between prayer and life is fundamentally the other side of the difference between God and the world that forms a constitutive element of faith. Prayer expresses man's recognition of God's divinity and this enables man at the same time to recognize his humanity. It is only where there is a space that is ultimately without purpose that man can resist the tendency to be dominated by purpose. In recognizing God's freedom, man is able to recognize his own freedom and to know where that space can be found. Prayer – and, with it, liturgy, meditation and contemplation as forms of prayer – constitutes an independent act on the part of man. This act in turn forms the basis of man's independence and that of the world. The ethical and practical imperative contained in the act of prayer does not, however, allow prayer to become totally functionalized. Prayer releases man both from the fatalism of the existing reality and from the fatalism of action. In every commitment to prayer, there is an inner release and recollectedness. These consequences of prayer are called joy and peace in the Bible. We may therefore conclude that prayer is the basis of man's truly human state.

Should we address God as a person in prayer? This question is more difficult than it seems at first sight. Is it possible to define prayer with a definition that is different from that used traditionally, that is, man's dialogue with God? We can, unfortunately, do no more than touch on the problems that arise when the category of person is applied to God. These problems are quite considerable. They were enunciated in a very radical form by Fichte in 1798, when the controversy with atheism was at its height. He showed that the concept of personality pointed to a distinction and

could not therefore be considered without reference to
finiteness. The problems that arise when the category
of person is not applied to God are even greater, however. Can the ultimate ground of man's existence be
an 'it' reality? If so, does this not lead to an extinction
of man's personality? Or is it not true to say that hope
of meaning and fulfilment is revealed to man's person
by the conviction that the depths of reality are
personal?

Both the Old and New Testaments bear witness to
one fundamental fact, namely that God is the one who
calls man, addresses him and leads him and deals in
sovereign and irreducible freedom with him. According to Scripture, God encounters us in the way in
which we encounter other persons. What other name
can we give, then, to God's way of speaking and acting
than this? We know how inadequate the category of
person is, but we have no other word that is more
suitable to express the testimony of Scripture.

Because God's way of dealing with man is personal,
man's response can therefore also only be personal.
This emerges quite clearly not only from the Old Testament and especially the psalms, but also from the
New Testament, which bears witness as firmly to the
use of 'Abba, Father' by the historical Jesus as a way
of addressing God as it does, for example, to Jesus'
solidarity with the poor and rejected. The word 'Abba'
seems to have been so highly valued in the early
Church that it was retained in the original Aramaic
idiom even in a Greek context (see, for example, Rom.
8.15; Gal. 4.6). The same applies to another early
Christian formula of prayer: 'Maranatha, come Lord!'
(1 Cor. 16:23; Acts 22:20; Did. 10:6), which is also a
personal form of address. Both these early Christian
prayer formulas also show that prayer, as personal
dialogue with God and Christ, has nothing to do with

an interior form of prayer based on a misunderstanding of the Sermon on the Mount and expressed by
going into one's room (Mt 6:6) and forgetting the
world. Both of these words are placed within an eschatological context and therefore within a universal
context. In both cases, it is a question of God's revelation of his divinity and, within this revelation, the
salvation of the world.

However much may be said on the justification of
prayer, the fact remains that it is a challenge to a
purely immanent way of thinking. It is therefore a
contradiction and it also evokes contradiction. Faith
and prayer can therefore be seen as a form of crisis
and this aspect is expressed in Scripture by the words
'conversion' and 'penance'. We can only understand
what this penance is if we see it against the background of an all-embracing understanding of faith. If
faith is turning to God without reservation, then it is
also turning away from other norms and other ways
of justifying and safeguarding one's life. It is turning
away from money, pleasure and power as ways of ful-
filling one's existence and finding security. If faith is
letting God be completely God and giving him honour,
then penance is a critical attitude in faith towards old
and new idols and all absolute claims made by ideological or political systems. Faith and penance are
therefore directly related to each other and the one
cannot be completely understood without reference to
the other. Penance is the other side or the negative
aspect of faith.

Faith is not synonymous with blindly trusting credulity or with a harmless and uncritical attitude.
There is no contradiction between faith and criticism.
The two belong indissolubly together. Faith without
a critical aspect becomes powerless and insipid. Faith
can therefore not be renewed either by preserving a

pre-critical attitude or by uncritically pursuing every new development. If it is to be renewed, its critical aspect – in other words, the aspect of conversion – has to be emphasized. No external renewal of the Church is possible if there is no inward renewal in the spirit of prayer and peace. One of the great tragedies of much of the attempted renewal in the Church today is that many Christians want the one without the other.

Notes

1. For the concept of faith, see J. Mouroux, *Ich glaube an Dich. Die personale Struktur des Glaubens* (Einsiedeln, 1951); M. Blondel, *Exigences philosophiques du christianisme* (Paris, 1950); J. Trütsch, 'Glaube und Erkenntnis', *Fragen der Theologie heute* (Einsiedeln & Cologne, 1957), pp. 45–68; *id.*, 'Glaube III', *Lexikon für Theologie und Kirche* IV² (1960), pp. 920–5; R. Aubert, *Le problème de l'acte de foi* (Louvain, ³1958); C. Cirne-Lima, *Der personale Glaube* (Innsbruck, 1959); H. Fries, *Glauben – Wissen. Wege zur Lösung des Problems* (Berlin, 1960); *id., Herausgeforderter Glaube* (Munich, 1968); M. Seckler, *Instinkt und Glaubenswille nach Thomas von Aquin* (Mainz, 1961); J. Pieper, *Über den Glauben* (Munich, 1962); G. Hasenhüttl, *Der Glaubensvollzug. Eine Begegnung mit Rudolf Bultmann aus katholischem Glaubensverständnisses* (Essen, 1963); U. Gerber, *Katholischer Glaubensbegriff* (Gütersloh, 1966); H. Bouillard, *Logik des Glaubens (Quaestiones disputatae 29)* (Freiburg, 1966); G. Muschalek, *Glaubensgewissheit in Freiheit (Quaestiones disputatae 40)* (Freiburg, 1968); J. Alfaro on faith in *Sacramentum Mundi* (1968).
2. H. Halbfas, *Fundamentalkatechetik. Sprache und Erfahrung im Religionsunterricht* (Düsseldorf, 1968), pp. 196, 198 ff, 207, 221 etc.
3. D. Sölle, *Atheistisch an Gott glauben. Beiträge zur Theologie* (Olten & Freiburg, 1968), pp. 82 ff.
4. For the biblical understanding of faith, see A. Schlatter, *Der Glaube im Neuen Testament* (Stuttgart, ⁴1927); A. Weiser & R. Bultmann, '*Pisteuo, pistis*' *Theologisches Wörterbuch zum Neuen Testament* VI (1959), pp. 174–230; R. Schnackenburg, 'Glaube I', *Lexikon für Theologie und Kirche* IV² (1960), pp. 913–7; J. Alfaro,

'Fides in terminologia biblica', *Gregorianum* 42 (1961), pp. 463–505.

5. G. Ebeling, 'Jesus and Glaube', *Wort und Glaube* I (Tübingen, 1960), pp. 239, 249.

6. M. Buber, *Zwei Glaubensweisen* (Zürich, 1950); Hans Urs von Balthasar, 'Zwei Glaubensweisen', *Spiritus creator* (Einsiedeln, 1967), pp. 76–91.

7. For the theology of prayer, see K. Rahner, *Worte ins Schweigen*, Innsbruck, 1928 ([8]1963); *id., Von der Not und dem Segen des Gebets* (Freiburg, 1958, [8]1968); *id.,* 'Vom Beten heute', *Geist und Leben* 42 (1969), pp. 6–17; *id.,* 'Thesen zum Thema "Glaube und Gebet" ', *op. cit.*, pp. 177–84; G. Ebeling, *Vom Gebet. Predigten über das Unser-Vater* (Tübingen, 1963); E. Schillebeeckx, *Personale Begegnung mit Gott* (Mainz, 1964); *id., Neues Glaubensverständnis* (Mainz, 1964); R. Schäfer, 'Gott und Gebet', *Zeitschrift für Theologie und Kirche* 65 (1965), pp. 117–28; J. Sudbrack on prayer in *Sacramentum Mundi* (1968); W. Bernet, *Gebet* (Stuttgart, 1970); O. H. Pesch, *Sprechender Glaube. Entwurf einer Theologie des Gebetes* (Mainz, 1970).

8. D. Sölle, *Atheistisch an Gott glauben, op. cit.*, p. 111.

9. J. A. T. Robinson, *Honest to God* (London, 1953).

10. G. Kittel, 'Abba', *Theologisches Wörterbuch zum Neuen Testament* I (1933), pp. 4–6; W. Marchel, *Abba, Père! La prière du Christ et des chrétiens. Etudes exégétiques sur les origines et la signification de l'invocation à la divinité comme père, avant et dans le Nouveau Testament (Analecta biblica* 19) (Rome, 1963); J. Jeremias, 'Abba', *Abba. Studien zur neutestamentlichen Theologie und Zeitgeschichte* (Gütersloh, 1966), pp. 15–66; *The Prayers of Jesus* (London, [4]1977); *id., Neutestamentliche Theologie* I (Gütersloh, 1971), pp. 67–73; G. Schrenk, 'Pater', *Theologisches Wörterbuch zum Neuen Testament* V (1954), pp. 946–1016; see also J. B. Metz, J. Moltmann & W. Oelmüller, *Kirche im Prozess der Aufklärung* (Munich & Mainz, 1970), pp. 74–8.

6 The content of faith

6.1 The confession of faith in the conflict of opinions

Asked about his faith, an average Christian would probably reply with a number of articles of faith. He would say, for example, that he believed that God existed and that he had revealed himself in Jesus Christ. He would also add that God founded the Church as the means of salvation. The contemporary crisis of faith that is so much discussed nowadays is usually interpreted as a crisis in the confession of certain articles or formulae of faith. Many members of the Church, it is widely believed, can no longer identify themselves with all that the Church confesses regarding faith.[1] We may conclude from this, then, that faith is defined on the basis of its content.

There is quite a strong movement against this today. Those who support this counter-movement, in which faith is radically questioned, are of the opinion that *what* the Christian believes in detail is less important than the fact *that* he believes at all and that he puts his faith into practice, both privately and in society. An objective content of faith is often seriously challenged by this movement and dismissed as an objectivization. Faith is also described as a way of understanding life and of expressing one's existence. Correct faith is sometimes defined not primarily as orthodoxy, but as orthopraxy. It is held that true and authentic faith is not to be found in correct formulae or definitions of faith, but in the correct practice of faith.

In this debate between orthodoxy and orthopraxy, there are, of course, broadly speaking the more conservative and the more progressive groups. The more conservative thinkers are concerned with the need to preserve faith as it had been handed down, whereas the progressives regard the realization of that faith in contemporary society as the most important task.

Although each side to some extent condemns the other as heretical, there is a very broad basis of agreement between them – much more than is generally recognized. The conservatives believe that traditional faith must be preserved because it is still of importance today. And why should the progressives concern themselves with the realization of faith if they were not convinced that that faith was truth and life for their fellow men? Both sides, then, share the same concern – the need to make faith present here and now.

Both points of view, however, have their dangers. In the search to make faith present in an up-to-date form, faith itself can be lost. On the other hand, in the anxiety to preserve traditional forms of faith, it is equally easy to lose sight of the modern world. The conservatives often seem to believe that what is important is how much the Christian believes and they often have a comprehensive list of questions and prepared answers available in order to test the orthodoxy of those with whom they are in discussion. But is it possible to count truths of faith like beads on a rosary? The progressives, on the other hand, seem to be predisposed to value highly the achievement of a good, open discussion. Public efficiency is usually regarded as very important and the most highly esteemed of all criteria of truth sometimes seems to be the published views of those who make public opinion.

As a theologian, I propose to question the normative content of faith by examining the normative documents of that faith – the Old and New Testaments. This method will, I think, provide us with a criterion which does not fit easily into the conservative or the progressive armoury, but which may show us the way out of our dilemma.

6.2 Faith in the history of salvation

Asked about their faith, the people of Israel did not reply with systematized statements about God, the world and man. Their answer took the form of a narrative, in which God's encounter with them in history and their experience of his faithful leadership were told. The Israelites were only able to confess faith in Yahweh because he had come to them in their history. Their faith, then, was a response to God's word. The fact that it was a response means that it was never an empty faith expressed as trust. It always had a concrete content.

The Old Testament faith was expressed in historical confessions of God's faithful and powerful activity in history and these formulae occur at quite an early period.[2] The earliest of all is the confession contained in the so-called oracles of Balaam: 'God brings them out of Egypt' (Num. 23.22 = 24.8). The decalogue is introduced by a similar formula, recalling God's leading the people out of Egypt (see Exod. 20:2; Dt. 5.6). A summary of the history of Israel's salvation in the form of a confession of faith is found in the Deuteronomist's 'short historical creed'. This passage con-

tains the most important events in Israel's history –
the call of Abraham, the liberation from slavery in
Egypt, from which Yahweh brought Israel 'with a
mighty hand and an outstretched arm, with great terror, with signs and wonders', and finally the occupa-
tion of the promised land. The response that the people
were to make was not simply that they should regard
these saving acts as true – they also had to express
their praise with an offering (see Deut. 26:5–10).

It was in the light of such experiences in history
that Israel came to understand who Yahweh was. The
verbal confessions of God's activity in Israel's history
therefore correspond to nominal confessions of Yahweh as the God of the people. The essential aspect of
Israel's faith is contained in the statement: 'Yahweh
is our God – we are his people' (see Deut. 26:16–19;
Hos. 2:24; Jer. 7:23; 31:33; Ezek. 11:20).

One of the distinctive aspects of the historical character of these confessions of faith in the Old Testament
is that they were reformulated and re-interpreted
quite often on the basis of new historical experiences.
A new understanding of faith was often gained in the
light of new experience and the new experiences were
also understood in the light of traditional faith. Such
new historical experiences always presented Israel
with a fresh challenge compelling the people to understand their faith in a new light. Israel's faith was
therefore in every respect a historical faith. The people
were always on the way with their faith. Their faith
was always restless and never closed. It was only in
the period of Judaism, the post-biblical period, that
this living, historical faith became a doctrinally formulated and inflexibly monotheistic confession: 'Hear,
Israel, your God is one' (Deut. 6:4).

Turning to the New Testament, we find that Jesus'
proclamation goes back beyond the rabbinical teach-

ing of his own period to the prophetic tradition, which
he makes more radical. The essence of Jesus' message
is that God is not remote, but present in the midst of
life. He avoided abstract formulae and used everyday,
living experiences as parables of God's actions. In sovereign freedom, Jesus placed himself above the 'tradition of the elders' (Mk 7:5) and taught 'as one who
had authority' (Mk 1:22). A confession of the immanent God was implicitly tied to the person of the earthly Jesus (see, for example, Mk 8:38). This power that
Jesus had to proclaim the immanent God was made
explicit after Easter. The connection between his person and the coming of the Kingdom of God that was
implicitly present in the earthly Jesus had to become
explicit after the Easter event and it is for this reason
that the post-paschal confessions of faith have a clear
Christological emphasis. Faith here is always faith in
Jesus Christ. This is why faith in the New Testament
has a content, which is not an abstract formula or
some anonymous depths of reality, but God himself.
This God is the God who spoke and acted in the history
of Jesus Christ. The content of New Testament faith
is therefore a person, his work and his fate.

This connection is clearly expressed in the earliest
confessions of faith made by the Christian community.[3] The early nominal confessions have the form:
'Jesus is the Kyrios' (Rom. 10:9; 1 Cor. 12:3) or 'Jesus
is the Christ' (1 Jn 2: 22; 5.1; 2 Jn 7). The most important formula, however, which later almost completely replaced all the others, was: 'Jesus is the Son
of God' (1 Jn 4:15; 5:5, etc.).

There are also several verbal formulas (*pistis formulae*) alongside these nominal formulae or homolo-
gies in the New Testament. This verbal confessions
speak of God's action in Jesus Christ, especially in the
cross and resurrection, and are not direct confessions

of the person of Jesus Christ himself. The confession
'that God raised him from the dead' (Rom. 10:9; see
also Acts 2:24, 32; 3:15, etc.; 1 Pet. 1:21, etc.) is a
verbal confession. The best known and most important
of these verbal confessions of faith is found in 1 Cor.
15:3–5: 'Christ died for our sins in accordance with the
scriptures; he was buried; he was raised on the third
day in accordance with the scriptures and he appeared
to Cephas, then to the twelve'. Paul introduced this
strophically structured formula as traditional and
made it the basis of his own theology.

Within the New Testament, then, there is a dogmatic tradition, but there is no unity of dogma. There
is, on the contrary, a great deal of variation between
the different formulae in which faith is confessed, de-
pending on the situation in which they are placed.
They are in each case determined by their *Sitz im
Leben* or existential location. They also attempt to
keep pace with the progress of reflection about faith.
A very important part is also played by historicity in
the New Testament confessions of faith. It was, for
example, not until the end of the New Testament
period, at the time when the pastoral epistles were
composed, that a much stronger emphasis came to be
laid on the preservation of the deposit of faith. It is in
these letters especially that the formula: 'The saying
is sure and worthy of full acceptance' (1 Tim. 1:15; 4:9)
is found. At this late period in the development of the
New Testament, the Word and formulation are
stressed more than at the beginning. Even so, the
limitations of a purely verbal orthodoxy are recognized
quite clearly: 'Even the demons believe and shudder'
(Jas 2.19). Even the devil can quote orthodox formu-
lations of faith, but what really matters is a living
faith (see Jas 2:17f).

We can therefore say that there are clearly formu-

lated confessions of faith in both the Old and the New
Testaments. In these, not only the individual believer,
but also the whole community of believers bear witness to their faith in a public and obligatory form.
These confessions call for a clear decision with regard
to wrong beliefs or lack of faith. They also display an
astonishing historical diversity. Nonetheless, they all
have one essential element in common – God's saving
activity in the history of man, which reaches a climax
in Jesus Christ. The nominal confessions or homolo-
gies speak of the person and the function of Jesus,
whereas the verbal or pistis formulae say that this
person was only who he was in the context of his
history. God's activity through the person and history
of Jesus Christ is therefore the central point of Christian faith. All the later proclamation of the Christian
message was related to this central aspect and had the
task of making it explicit and present.

Because of this task, the history of the confession of
faith that began in the New Testament cannot be regarded as having ended with the completion of the
canon. A pure biblicism would hardly be in accordance
with the historical and universal character of Christian faith. The history of the canon of the New Testament, then, led directly into the history of dogma.
The basic structure of the apostolic confession of faith
as we know it today developed from beginnings that
had already been made in the New Testament. Its
original structure in the beginning of the third century
AD arose from questions put to those seeking baptism.[4] Its present form, however, did not emerge until
the eighth and ninth centuries. Alongside this western
text, there were also confessions in the East. One of
these, which was probably the confession used by the
community of Caesarea, became the framework into
which the dogmatic definitions of the two first ecu-

menical councils of Nicaea (325) and Constantinople (381) were fitted. It was in this way that the longer Nicene creed was formed. Its basic structure is clearly characterized by the history of salvation, which is why the dogmatic formula of the later Council of Chalcedon (451), dealing with the one person in two natures of Jesus Christ, was not introduced into it. In any case, the definition of Chalcedon is quite different from the so-called Nicene creed. This is clear from the introduction, which is not formulated as 'we confess' or 'we believe', but as 'we teach that it must be confessed'. The confession that has developed in the course of the history of salvation has here become a right teaching of the confession. A formula of confession has become a dogmatic teaching formula.

This tendency continued in the later history of dogma. The one all-embracing content of faith came more and more to be developed in its individual aspects, implications and conclusions. These attempts to make faith explicit in dogmatic statements came about in the first place not as the result of a inner need to speculate, but rather because of practical needs. Faith had to be defined again and again as new and heretical misunderstandings arose. The negative aspect of this tendency to make dogmatic pronouncements, however, was the increasing danger of the one faith becoming buried beneath more and more articles of faith. It became more difficult, even impossible, to see the wood of faith for the dogmatic trees.

6.3 Concentration rather than reduction

It is hardly surprising that, in this difficult situation, a counter-tendency arose in the modern era. Attempts were made to replace the system of explicitating faith in dogmatic statements by a reduction of faith to its essential content. The movement to find the 'essence of Christianity'[5] began as early as the Middle Ages and was notably strong in late mediaeval mysticism. It continued with increasing insistence in humanism, pietism and the Enlightenment. In this movement, a distinction was made between fundamental truths of faith which, for the sake of salvation, had to be believed by all, and truths which were not fundamental and which could therefore be left open to the free consent of individual believers. In his encyclical letter, *Mortalium animos*, of 1928, Pius XI opposed these attempts to reduce faith with the argument that the authority of God was present in all articles of faith, with the result that the dogma of the immaculate conception of Mary, for example, had to be accepted as firmly as the mystery of the Trinity and that the incarnation of God had to be believed in accordance with the teaching of the magisterium. Any questioning of God's authority in a particular point, the Pope argued, amounted to a total denial of that authority. The aim of the encyclical was to remove officially all danger of a reduction of the living historical faith of Christianity to a few abstract and plain statements that were regarded as universally essential.

This magisterial attempt to solve the problem was, however, far from successful. A high price had to be paid for the defence of the Catholic and all-embracing aspect of Christian faith. The living faith of Christianity had in fact become a closed system of plain statements and the whole system had either to be swallowed in one piece or else questioned in detail or as a whole. The network of dogmatic pronouncements had become so tight that the system was no longer open to receive the new historical situation of faith in the modern world.

A one-sided presentation of the formally obligatory character of each individual dogma on the basis of the authority of God and the Church inevitably had a fatal effect in the modern era, with its emphasis on subjectivity. The subject was bound to ask: 'Can I believe in the central Christological truth with the same subjective intensity as I believe in the Marian dogmas?' The question of salvation or its absence is not involved in the same way in Christology and Mariology and the same degree of subjective commitment is therefore not possible.

This placing of equal emphasis on all Christian teaching also led to a fatal change in equilibrium in the proclamation of the Christian message and in pious practice. The image of the Church in the modern era became to a very great extent characterized by an emphasis on secondary and even tertiary aspects. A much too heavy emphasis was placed during and after the Counter-reformation on anti-Protestant truths and this led to an over-accentuation of truths concerned with the means of salvation, such as the Church, the sacraments and offices, and a neglect of Christological and soteriological truths throughout the modern era. In the nineteenth and even in the present century, more encyclicals were written on the subject of Mariology than on such questions as Christology or even the pressing claims of atheism. This imbalance is a clear sympton of the malfunctioning of the heart and circulation of Christianity. The one-sided insistence on verbal and formal orthodoxy is at least partly responsible for the failure of Christianity to reach sufficient people in the modern era.

Catholic theologians have, in recent years, often debated whether a movement back to greater concentration ought not to be initiated, after such a long period in which faith has been made explicit in dogmatic

102 AN INTRODUCTION TO CHRISTIAN FAITH

pronouncements and the consequences of this process have in many cases been disastrous. Concentration here does not imply a reduction or an elimination, nor does it point to a demythologizing attempt to produce an insipid essential formula by means of distillation. It is much more a question of making the one faith clear in the many articles of faith and of distinguishing what is peripheral from what is central. This need for concentration is justified in one of the most important documents of the second Vatican Council. In its statement about the hierarchy of truths, the Decree on Ecumenism declared: 'When comparing doctrines, they (= Catholic theologians) should remember that in Catholic teaching there exists an order or a hierarchy of truths, since they vary in their relationship to the foundation of Christian faith'. The decree goes on to indicate that this foundation is to be found in the 'unfathomable riches of Christ' (Eph. 3:8).[6] In the preparatory work leading up to the acceptance of the final text, it was suggested that the truths of faith ought to be considered rather than counted up.

According to this conciliar text, then, a quantitative and formal understanding of truth has to be replaced by a qualitative understanding determined by the content of truth. It would be a complete misunderstanding of this doctrine of the hierarchy of truths and an obvious continuation of quantitative rather than qualitative thinking if we were to believe that the individual truths of faith could still be numbered and in this way separated into more important and less important truths. Correctly understood, this doctrine points to the fact that the content of faith is not simply the sum total of individual statements, but a structured whole obeying certain laws of proportion.

There are two obvious consequences of this new orientation in the presentation of faith. The first is the possibility of what have been called short or abbreviated formulae of faith.[7] These represent an attempt to express the singleness and wholeness of faith in a short, striking way, without omitting or denying any aspect of faith. The biblical confessions of faith and the Apostles' Creed were short formulae of this type which made it possible for justice to be done to faith in a very comprehensive summary. The believer who confesses that God in Jesus Christ was the salvation and hope of all men is confessing not a part, but the whole of Christian faith, even though he is not necessarily understanding all the consequences that the Church has drawn from this statement in the course of almost two thousand years.

The secondary consequence of this concentration of faith is that there are not only formal criteria, such as scripture, tradition and the magisterium, by which faith can be correctly understood, but also material criteria and material criticism. This material criterion was summarized by Luther in the formula: 'What drives Christ', which revealed the Christological meaning of all pronouncements about faith. It is only when they can be understood Christologically that statements about faith, even including the Marian dogmas, are theologically correct and legitimate.

It is, of course, important for this material principle not to be a selective principle, but a principle of interpretation. What is more, it is not only the most important aspect that is really important. It may even be – and has indeed often been in the history of the Church – that fundamental principles have been resolved on the basis of relatively peripheral questions. At the Council of Ephesus in 431, for example, the true incarnation of God was discussed on the basis of the title 'God-bearer' (*Theotokos*'). The so-called peripheral truths should therefore not be treated with indifference. On the other hand, it is important for peripheral questions not to be allowed to block the way to the centre and obscure it. The essential aspect of this process of concentration is that the one Word of God should be audible among the many words.

6.4 Structural analysis of the confession of faith

If these new emphases are to be more than empty suggestions, we must face the task of analyzing the content of faith structurally in broad outline and, taking the Christological centre of faith as our point of departure, look at the whole of Christian faith.

The fundamental structure of faith is expressed clearly in scripture and the Apostles' Creed.[8] The latter makes a clear distinction between *credere in Deum, in Jesus Christum, in Spiritum Sanctum* on the one hand and *credere ecclesiam* on the other. The Church and all that accompanies it, particularly the sacraments and offices, are believed in a different way from God, who acts in Jesus Christ and through the Holy Spirit for our salvation. It is to God alone that faith is directly related and it is God who forms the real content of that faith. The Church, together with its sacraments and offices, is only a means of salvation and faith is related to it to the extent that it mediates salvation and makes it present. The Christian therefore does not believe in the Church – or the pope, for example – in the same way that he believes in God. The means of salvation have to be seen as ways in which salvation is mediated and, if they are no longer satisfactorily performing this function, they should be criticized.

It is possible to throw even more light on the fundamental structure of faith if we take the difference between the truths of the aim or end and the truths of the means of salvation as our point of departure.[9] Let us begin by making a distinction between the truths of the aim or end. It is possible, for example, to distinguish between the statements of faith themselves and reflection about these statements. A statement of faith is a confession of God's saving activity in Jesus Christ through the Holy Spirit. This confession of the Trinity within the economy of salvation is different from the immanent Trinity itself. Statements about the immanent Trinity or the pre-existence of Christ who are not really direct statements of faith at all, but theological reflections expressed as statements. They aim, in a heightened reflection, to say in a different way what has already been said in the direct confession of God's actvity in and through Jesus Christ. They aim, in other words, to keep firmly to the historical irreducibility of the Christian faith by 'making it firm' in God's eternity. The doctrine of the Trinity aims to express what is outside us, the fact that salvation is already given to us in Christ. God can only be life and love that communicates itself to us in history because he *is* in himself that life and love. All that the doctrine of the Trinity says, then, is that God has revealed himself in Christ as the one who he *is*. The statements about the Trinity therefore say nothing new with regard to the content, but make the original statement of faith explicit in metaphysical language.

It is therefore possible to make the Christological confession positively explicit. In the same way, it is also possible to explicitate it in the negative sense. The Christological statement that God wants to save the whole world in Jesus Christ at the same time implies the negative statement that there is no salvation outside Christ and that the world lacks salvation without him. If it is separated from a way of understanding that is historically conditioned, the doctrine of original sin is no more than the negative expression of a positive statement. It can be understood in this sense even today and indeed, if the Christological truth is not to be called radically into question, it is a completely indispensable doctrine. It is, however, not a new or additional truth, but simply a negative expression of a central confession of Jesus as the salvation of the world.

Like the statements about the aim or end of salvation, those about the means of salvation can also be individually formulated. The Council of Trent provided us with the fundamental standpoint for such statements by declaring that the sacraments – and similarly the Church's offices – could be given a concrete form by the Church, *salva illorum substantia*, according to the needs of the age.[10] A distinction, in other words, was made between the substance and the concrete historical form. What that substance was continued to be disputed among theologians. Even in the traditional theology, there are different interpretations, such as the point of view that Christ instituted the sacraments only *in genere*, in other words, in accordance with a universal idea. In the light of contemporary historical insights, a broad rather than a narrow point of view would have to be adopted today with regard to this question, since we know with greater precision today that the sacraments and offices occur in very specifically socially conditioned forms in scripture. For this reason, the forms that we have of the sacraments and the offices in the New Testament and the earliest tradition of the Church can be no more than models. They cannot therefore simply be imitated today, but have to be given a contemporary form in the light of relationships and pastoral needs. The Church's essential substance is never in a chemically pure state. It only exists in concrete historical forms. In giving a later dogmatic expression to these forms which had become historical and which had therefore not existed from the beginning in historically concrete forms, the Church did not intend to say any more than that it was the Church of Jesus Christ in this concrete form.

This thesis is important for our understanding of many of the Church's dogmas. It should not alarm us to recall that it was not until the twelfth century that the Church began to think in terms of seven sacraments and that it was many centuries later, roundabout the time of the first Vatican Council, that clarity was reached with regard to the question of papal primacy. In regarding these truths today as dogmas and submitting them not only as *fides ecclesiastica*, the faith of the Church, with the obligation to obey the Church, but also as *fides divina*, divine faith, the Church does not basically intend to say any more than that this concrete Church, with this concrete form in its sacraments and offices, is in substantial continuity with the apostolic beginning of the Church and is the one divine means of salvation for the world.

The Church does not intend, with these and similar dogmas, to claim that the history of dogma may not have developed quite differently. What it does, however, claim is that the way in which the history of dogma has in fact developed in no sense points to a break with continuity from the beginning and that the Church is the historically obligatory form in which the truth of Jesus Christ and salvation come to us. All the many different pronouncements about the Church, its sacraments and its offices can in fact be concentrated into the one single statement, namely that God wants the Church in concrete to be the one sign and the means of salvation for the world. The sacraments and the offices are ways in which the Church expresses itself. It articulates its essential being in them [11] The Church can, however, only preserve its identity by means of historical change in the way in which this articulation takes place.

I must now consider very briefly one more group of truths. Both the truths of the aim or end and the truths of the means of salvation are accompanied by paradigmatic or typological truths. The Mariological dogmas are of this kind. Their function is to express other truths in a symbolical, exemplary and typological way. The two earliest Mariological dogmas, Mary's motherhood of God and her virginity, thus contain Christological truths. In their own way, they point to the fact that God entered our human history in Christ and in this manner made a new beginning from below as it were and through 'flesh and blood'. They thus bear witness to Jesus Christ as the second Adam. The two most recent Mariological dogmas, the immaculate conception and the assumption of Mary into heavenly glory, exemplify ecclesiological and soteriological statements. Mary is presented as the type of the Church and redeemed mankind. We are told through her example, as though in an image, what God has in store for man and what he intends to make of man. The Marian dogmas, then, are not additional, as far as their content is concerned, to the central Christological dogma, but the typological exemplification of that central truth.

6.5 The one theme: correct speaking about God and man

At first sight, the structural analysis that I have just carried out gives a very complicated impression. The result, on the other hand, is extremely simple. Despite the great number and complexity of historical statements and the different ways in which these pronouncements have been formulated, the same faith is revealed in its singleness and unity. Each article of faith expresses a different perspective of this one, whole faith. It is like a fugue in which the same theme is the subject of many different variations, and only reveals its inner richness and fulness in this variation and composition. The one continuous theme of the history of dogma is none other than the theme of Jesus' proclamation: God's rule as the salvation of mankind. God's cause and mankind's cause became one in the person and work of Jesus Christ. Therefore the Christological concentration of all pronouncements of faith should not be understood too narrowly. It is the essential concept and summary of what God means for man and man means for God. Therefore the divine existence of God as the basis of the humanity of man revealed and realized in Jesus Christ is the one word in many words, and the one dogma in many dogmas. Whoever affirms and acknowledges that God in Jesus Christ is salvation, hope and peace for all mankind, and whoever commits himself to that affirmation in order to become a figure of hope for others, believes and affirms the whole Christian faith, because that whole faith is not a whole made up of dogmatic statements, but the wholeness of a person: Jesus the Christ.

This Christological unity of all pronouncements of faith offers two important consequences for the interpretation of truths of faith. First: Christological interpretation is theological and doxological interpretation. Jesus Christ is the way to the Father (cf. Jn 14:6). The Christological formulae do not therefore remain as it were self-satisfied, but extend beyond themselves and transcend themselves in and into the no longer describable mystery of God. The 'through Christ to God' (*per Christum in Deum*) notion has methodological and hermeneutical consequences for theology. Aquinas understood this point when he put it thus: *actus autem credentis non terminatur ad enuntiabile, sed ad rem* – faith does not stop at what can be said, but at the matter itself.[12] This *res*, this matter or 'cause' of faith is for Aquinas *Deus sub ratione Deitatis*, the divinity of God about which we know more in regard to what it is not, than in regard to what it is.[13] Hence: *articulus est perceptio divinae veritatis tendens in ipsam.*[14] The article of faith is a real conception of divine truth, it is not a mere cypher. But it is a conception which extends beyond itself into what is no longer conceivable. Any superficial claim to know it all and any clever emphasis on particular formulae is excluded. Ultimately dogma is doxology. Its proper existential location (*Sitz im Leben*) is liturgical and devotional profession and confession of faith.

Second: Christological interpretation is anthropological and 'secular' interpretation. I shall say more about this when I come to discuss the salvific dimension of faith. Here I shall say only that dogma has to take effect as a form of the Gospel, as an assertion of salvation to mankind. Dogma was inadequately explained when it was used only to prevail over others in the sense that it alone led redemption. Dogmas are to be interpreted as a form of glad tidings and not as ill tidings. They must be interpreted so that they can be understood as the offer of a more human form of human existence. Only thus can they become a challenge binding on conscience and a challenge to life and death.

Hence, finally: The content of faith is a call to a decision to adopt Jesus' cause, which is the cause of God with mankind. This critical nature of faith can be diminished and neutralized in two ways. The content of dogmas can be watered down until they are no more than a few general human clichés. But it is also possible to radicalize faith, and to make it so sublime by means of iconoclastic demythologization, that it is quite without any content at all. That kind of formal interpretation seems to demand everything and in reality is not demanding at all. In reality it is inconsequential and not binding in the least. Both positions are only apparently progressive. Without the 'factual reference' of a dogma, faith becomes formless and faceless; it lacks reality and seriousness. A faith without content is non-objective. In this respect it is not a matter of conservative or progressive. It is solely a question of whether faith acknowledges the standard and measure that we encounter in Jesus Christ. It is simply a question of whether faith stays Christian; of whether it takes Jesus Christ as its basis, and says how we are to talk in an appropriately Christian manner about God and about mankind.

Notes

1. For the problem of the confession of faith, see P. Brunner, G. Friedrich, K. Lehmann & J. Ratzinger, *Veraltetes Glaubensbekenntnis?* (Regensburg, 1968); *Concilium* I (1970), which deals with 'Tension between Church and Faith', especially Morris L. West, 'Causes of Disquiet in the Church', *op. cit.*, pp. 13–20.
2. For the Old Testament confessions of faith, see G. von Rad, 'Das formgeschichtliche Problem des Hexateuch', *Gesammelte Schriften zum Alten Testament* (Munich ³1965), pp. 9–86; J. Schreiner, in *Concilium* 2 (1966); W. Richter, 'Beobachtungen zur theologischen Systembildung in der alttestamentlichen Literatur anhand des "Kleinen geschichtlichen Credo"', *Wahrheit und Verkündigung (Festschrift für M. Schmaus)* (Munich, 1967), pp. 175–212; E. Zenger, 'Funktion und Sinn der ältesten Herausforde-

rungsformel', *Zeitschrift der deutschen morgenländischen Gesellschaft*, Supplement 1 (1969), pp. 334–42.
3. For the New Testament confessions of faith, see O. Cullmann, *Die ersten christlichen Glaubensbekenntnisse* (Theologische Studien 15), (Zürich, ²1949); V. H. Neufeld, *The Earliest Christian Confessions (New Testament Toles and Studies 5) (Leiden, 1963);* E. Schweizer, *Erniedrigung und Erhöhung bei Jesus und seinen Nachfolgern* (Zürich, 1962), pp. 87–109; W. Kramer, *Christos, Kyrios, Gottessohn* (Zürich, 1963); H. Conzelmann, *Grundriss der Theologie des Neuen Testaments* (Munich, 1967), pp. 81–112; K. Lehmann, *Auferweckt am dritten Tag nach der Schrift. Früheste Christologie, Bekenntnisbildung und Schriftauslegung im Lichte von 1 Kor 15, 3–5* (Quaestiones disputatae 38) (Freiburg, 1968); H. Schlier, 'Die Anfänge des christologischen Credo', *Zur Frühgeschichte der Christologie* (Quaestiones disputatae 51) (Freiburg, 1970), pp. 13–58.
4. The texts will be found not only in Denzinger-Schönmetzer 1–76, but in A. Hahn, *Bibliothek der Symbole und Glaubensregeln der alten Kirche* (Breslau, 1897). A selection, translated into German and with a commentary, will also be found in the volume edited by H. Steubing, *Bekenntnisse der Kirche. Bekenntnistexte aus zwanzig Jahrhunderten* (Wuppertal, 1970). There are also a number of fundamental historical investigations into these texts, the most notable being F. Kattenbusch, *Das apostolische Symbol* (Leipzig, 1894); A. Seeberg, *Der Katechismus der Urchristenheit* (Leipzig, 1903); H. Lietzmann, *Kleine Schriften III* (Berlin, 1962), pp. 163–281; J. N. D. Kelly, *Early Christian Creeds* (London, 1950); J. de Ghellinck, *Patristique et Moyen-âge. Etudes d'histoire littéraire et doctrinale I* (Paris, 1949). More recent interpretations have been provided by J. Ratzinger, *Introduction to Christianity* (London, 1969); H. de Lubac, *La Foi chrétienne. Essai sur la structure du Symbole des Apôtres* (Paris, 1969).
5. For the history of the question of the 'essence of Christianity', see C. H. Ratschow, *'Christentum V', Religion in Geschichte und Gegenwart* I³ (1957), pp. 1712–29; R. Schäfer, 'Welchen Sinn hat es nach einem Wesen des Christentums zu suchen?', *Zeitschrift für Theologie und Kirche* 65 (1968), pp. 329–47. The most important contribution was made by A. von Harnack, *Das Wesen des Christentums* (Leipzig, 1900) (reprinted Munich & Hamburg, 1964, with an introduction by R. Bultmann). The Catholic contributions to this question include M. Schmaus, *Vom Wesen des Christentums* (Wertheim, 1947); R. Guardini, *Das Wesen des Christentums* (Würzburg, ⁵1958); Karl Adam, *Das Wesen des Katholizismus*

(Düsseldorf, [13]1957); K. Rahner, 'Christentum', *Lexikon für Theologie und Kirche* II² (1958), pp. 1100–15; *id., Sacramentum Mundi* I (1967); J. Ratzinger, *Vom Sinn des Christseins* (Munich, 1965); H. Schlier, *Das bleibende Katholische. Ein Versuch über ein Prinzip des Katholischen* (Münster, 1970). 6. For the hierarchy of truths, see the Decree on Ecumenism of Vatican II, *Unitatis Redintegratio*, II. See also J. Feiner, 'Das Zweite Vatikanische Konzil II', *Lexikon für Theologie und Kirche* (1968), pp. 88–90; H. Mühlen, 'Die Lehre des Vatikanum II über die "hierarchia veritatum" und ihre Bedeutung für den ökumenischen Dialog', *Theologie und Glaube* 56 (1966), pp. 303–35; U. Valeske, *Hierarchia veritatum. Theologiegeschichtliche Hintergründe und mögliche Konsequenzen eines Hinweises im Ökumenismusdekret des II. Vatikanischen Konzils zum zwischenkirchlichen Gespräch* (Munich, 1968); W. Kasper, 'Zum Problem der Rechtgläubigkeit in der Kirche von morgen', *Kirchliche Lehre – Skepsis der Gläubigen* (Freiburg, 1970), pp. 66–72.
7. See K. Rahner, in *Theological Investigations* (London, 1969); K. Lehmann, 'Bemühungen und eine "Kurzformel" des Glaubens,' *Herderkorrespondenz* 23 (1969), pp. 32–8; *id.,* 'Zum Problem einer Konzentration der Glaubensaussagen', *'Kurzformel des Glaubens und seiner Verkündigung', Rechenschaft vom Glauben*, eds., E. Hesse & H. Erharter, (Vienna, 1969), pp. 117–35; H. Küng, 'Was ist die christliche Botschaft?', *Die Zukunft der Kirche. Berichtband des Concilium-Kongresses 1970* (Zürich & Mainz, 1971), pp. 78–86; R. Bleistein, *Kurzformel des Glaubens* (Würzburg, 1971); A. Stock, *Kurzformeln des Glaubens. Zur Unterscheidung des Christlichen bei Karl Rahner* (Einsiedeln & Cologne, 1971).
8. See P. Nautin, *Je crois à l'Esprit Saint dans la sainte Eglise pour la résurrection de la chair (Unam sanctam 17)* (Paris, 1947).
9. See Thomas Aquinas, *Summa Theologiae* II/II, q. 6, a. 1.
10. Denzinger-Schönmetzer 1728 = new series 426.
11. See K. Rahner, *The Church and the Sacraments (Quaestiones disputatae)* (London, 1963). In Rahner's theology, this concept is, however, connected with a theory of the irreversible evolution of the Church. Neither the critical superiority and normative nature of the apostolic beginning of the Church nor the historicity of the Church are, however, guaranteed in this approach. See J. Neumann, 'Das "Ius divinum" im Kirchenrecht', *Orientierung* 31 (1967), pp. 5–8. For the solution by means of a model concept that is suggested here, see W. Kasper, 'Zum Problem

der Rechtgläubigkeit in der Kirche von morgen', *op. cit.*, pp. 73 and note 60.

12. Thomas Aquinas, *Summa theologiae* II/II q. 1 a. 2 ad 2.

13. *Ibid.*, q. 1 a. 1

14. *Ibid.*, q. 1 1. 6.

7 Faith and salvation

7.1. Salvation in and/or beyond the world

One of the main features of the present situation of faith is that the questions coming up for discussions are not just so-called borderline ones. They are not just the questions which arise between theology and the natural sciences, psychology and sociology. Of course these borderline problems continue to exist, and in many ways they have become more urgent. But the problems faced by theology go much deeper. What is in question today is not just the edges of the Christian faith, but the centre. Even such central and fundamental kerygmatic terms as grace, salvation and redemption are for many people today little more than empty formulas, meaningless relics of an obsolete religious language with nothing to say to human experience as we know it. Many regard them as expressions of an age in which human beings had not yet come to full responsibility for their lives. Quite often they were used to off-load responsibility for ourselves and our world on to a *Deus ex machina*. That is why modern criticis of ideology, most recently J. Kahl in his pamphlet on 'The Poverty of Christianity',[1] have seen them as bearing the main responsibility for the disarray and inhumanity of our society. If we start from the premiss that we must find our own solutions to the problems facing us, what sense can we still give to the term 'redemption'? Doesn't this belief in redemption force us to live simultaneously in two worlds? In a world dominated by rationality, calculation and practicability what room is left for grace? Is such a supernaturalism still viable?

These are questions and not answers. But they are questions we must take seriously. We must take them seriously because they pick up Christianity on its own claim to be not *just* belief in invisible and other-worldly realities, but saving faith.[2] The Christian faith does not set out to be just a set of opinions, not just a worldview or an interpretation of the world. The word preached as scripture understands it is not just an interpretation of existence, and certainly not mere information; it is a living (Acts 7:38; Heb. 4:12; 1 Pet. 1:23) and an active (Ps. 147:15ff; Heb. 4:12) word. Faith therefore regards itself as the basis and beginning of saved existence for man and his world. 'For man believes with his heart and so is justified, and he confesses with his lips and is saved' (Rom. 10:10; cf. Acts 16:31). Yes, faith even claims to be the only channel through which a human being receives the righteousness of God (cf. Rom. 1:16–17; 3:22). That is why the Council of Trent says that faith is the beginning, basis and root of justification,[3] that is, of proper human existence. It is only in these soteriological terms, in relation to human salvation, that faith can be adequately expressed.

But what is salvation? What do we mean when we talk about redemption? When scripture talks about grace and salvation it uses a whole multitude of concepts and images to define the reality which is salvation from the largest possible number of positions: life, light, peace, freedom, reconciliation, justification, sanctification, redemption, kingdom, love, hope, joy,

and so on. In other words, scripture makes no attempt
to capture the reality of salvation in a single abstract
concept or dogmatic definition. Instead it starts from
quite real experiences and situations: illness, the danger of death, imprisonment, servitude, war, argument,
in which the absence of salvation in existence is obvious. In these situations a human being realizes that
he does not belong completely to himself, that he has
been dispossessed of himself and his world and sold
into the power of forces which he himself cannot master. In this plight he turns to God, for human salvation
does not consist in some graces distinct from God, but
in God himself (cf. Is. 12:2; 35:4 etc.). It is a characteristic of the terms and images we have mentioned
that they do not address themselves just to a man or
woman's spiritual, purely interior and personal dimension, but envisage the single, whole person, and
include his or her physical and public dimension. We
are not therefore talking about a super-nature which
can be sharply distinguished from nature. we are talking about overcoming the alienations which make our
existence unfree,[4] and about the reality of an authentic, fulfilled existence. We are concerned with the holiness and wholeness of a human being in and with his
world.

This broad conception of salvation was lost in the
theology of recent centuries as a result of various historical developments in knowledge in general and theology in particular. As modern science advanced in its
understanding of the natural causes of things, so theology and preaching retreated to the quiet waters of
the supernatural. In the seventeenth century Ripalda
even talked about an *ens supernaturale*, and in the
nineteenth century J. M. Scheeben invented the noun
'super-nature' from what had previously been the only
form, the adjective 'supernatural'. Neo-scholasticism

defined the relation of nature and super-nature purely negatively, as one of non-contradiction; the internal connection and mutual relation of the two was lost. This is how the much discussed two-storey model of nature and super-nature developed, which could not be superseded until our century, as a result of the stimulus of the French *théologie nouvelle* (Henri de Lubac, H. Bouillard) after the second World War.[5]

Such a view of nature and grace as externally related contradicts the basic message of Scripture. The canon of Scripture was compiled in the second century in the dispute with Marcion. Marcion wanted to separate the Old Testament from the New Testament, the creator God from the redeemer God. The Church's insistence on including the Old Testament as well as the New Testament in the scriptural canon was based on the fundamental decision that creation and redemption belong together. We can go so far as to say that the unity of creation and redemption is *the* canonical truth of scripture and as such *the* hermeneutical principle of scriptural exegesis. If the order of salvation were no longer to be connected with the order of creation, this would be a denial of the universality of redemption. It was for this reason that the first Vatican Council condemned, not only naturalism and rationalism, but supernaturalism and fideism, and declared the interrelation of 'natural' and 'supernatural' revelation to be a fundamental principle for interpreting revelation.[6] The connection between creation and redemption was illustrated in a second incident from the history of the early Church. The Christological disputes of the first centuries were not just about the true divinity of Jesus; much more dangerous in the second and third centuries were the heresies which denied the true humanity of Jesus. When, in the controversy with docetism and gnosticism, the

Church defended the true and full humanity of Jesus, it was trying to say that salvation comes to us in human form and in a human form, that the salvation Christianity talks about is human salvation. It was trying to say that God is a God of human beings and comes to human beings in human ways.

For us today the disputes of that time are not just history. In reaction against a one-sided horizontalism, that is, in reaction against a reduction of Christianity to human fellowship and social criticism, there is currently a danger of something like a new supernaturalism. People think that by insisting that salvation does not come from below, but from above, they can block these tendencies and also defend the hierarchical structure of the Church. If this supernaturalism were to prevail, the Church would become a sect, living on alongside society, but without any communication with it. Its message of salvation would then inevitably appear as an ideological superstructure and idle hope. However, if we take seriously the Christological decisions of the early Church about the true and full humanity of Jesus, then there is no theology from above without a corresponding theology from below. Any understanding of God and salvation which left out the world would necessarily lead to an understanding of the world which had no place for God or salvation. This requires us to have a 'secular' interpretation of the faith, in the proper sense of the term. That does not mean that the world as such is the criterion for a correct understanding of the faith, but it does mean that it must be a point of reference, indeed the central point of reference, for any Christian understanding of salvation.

7.2. The advance of political theology

The task of rethinking the Christian understanding of salvation in a secular context has been undertaken in our time primarily by political theology.[7] The concerns of this movement are much more serious and much wider than the clumsy and misleading term 'political theology' implies. Political theology should not be identified with the 'theology of revolution'. Nor does it set out to be a politicizing theology and reproduce on the left the old integrism of the right. Lastly, it is not a system of political ethics attempting to produce a political or social programme. It is concerned rather with examining all theological statements for their social relevance. Social relevance, because political theology regards society as man's widest context. It is the essence of reality as this presents itself to us in the conditions of the modern period. To communicate the faith in secular terms, involved with this reality, therefore means to express it in a way which has relevance to society, to put it into words and translate it into practice in such a way that it helps social reality to attain salvation. As a result of this conception political theology does not see itself as just one area of theology, but a general new approach to doing theology.

The theological premises of political theology to a large extent dominate current discussions. It is an area in which opinions are at present divided. This means that we shall have to deal in detail with this position when we are discussing the question of the significance of faith for salvation. Let us start by looking at the arguments political theology uses in its support. The first argument normally put forward is that the individual Christian and the Church already exist, before they take any political position or action, within a network of political and social relations. Before the Church takes a position on a political issue, it already occupies a political position by being an institution in society. Therefore, if the Church is not to be covertly saddled with political ideologies, it has no way of avoiding a critical examination of the political implications of all its pronouncements. Even political absention can in certain circumstances be a political position and serve as a cloak for existing injustice. The Church thus cannot avoid the political dimension. Not to accept this is either shortsighted or, alternatively, amounts to obscuring actual positions of power and domination. There is therefore no such thing as a totally non-political theology, and a mere withdrawal from everyday events is no criterion for the seriousness of theology.

A second argument deals with more fundamental questions. It starts from the question of the nature of the reality in terms of which we have to articulate our faith today. Today it is clearly not a given nature, a universe which encompasses us, but a reality which human labour, civilization and technology are helping to shape. Human activity is a constitutive element in the make-up of this reality. This reality is mediated through society. To proclaim the faith so that it speaks to this reality means today to articulate it in socially relevant terms. This is only possible, however, if theology rethinks the relationship of theory and practice. Faith must become practical in order to reach reality. Only in and through practice does it realize its identity. In all this political theology does not see itself as borrowing a currently fashionable view of reality. Far from it, it is convinced that this view is in accord with the attitude of the Bible. Part of the meaning of truth in the biblical sense is that it must be done (cf. Jn 3:21). Truth must be upheld, not just before private

conscience, but also in a public legal dispute. Only
then is it in accord with Jesus' original message of the
basileia. It would also be a misunderstanding of Paul
to accuse him – as is often done – of a spiritualization
of the Old Testament and Synoptic message. The
freeing of the Christian message from its ties with a
specific political nation does not for him mean a retreat
to private conscience, but the universal mission, the
bringing in of all the nations. To ask about the social
efficacy of faith is therefore a quite proper theological
question.

We must, then, take the concerns of political theology seriously and examine them seriously. On the
other hand, we cannot accept the proposed framework
as satisfactory. In many respects it is too narrow and
therefore leads inevitably – even if this is not the
intention of the proponents of political theology – to a
diminishing of the Christian message. Consider only
the headings 'prayer' and 'sacrament', which clearly
cannot be given an adequate theological description
solely within social dimensions. This is not to say that
prayer and sacrament do not also have a social dimension, but that they are not exhausted by it and that
therefore a broader theological approach is necessary
to take account of the significance of faith for salvation. Let me first offer two arguments for this view,
one more philosophical and one more theological.

Philosophically we must first agree with political
theology that human freedom is real freedom in Hegel's sense. It is not enough to talk in purely abstract
terms about a freedom which belongs to the essence of
a human being, a freedom which even a prisoner possesses because his thoughts are free and he can choose
which corner of his cell he is going to sit in. To talk
about freedom in such an abstract way can be a down-
right insult to a person's real lack of freedom. In a real

and humanly complete form, freedom is only possible in the association and interaction of persons. Real freedom therefore has social preconditions. It is only possible when it is not suppressed or infringed by the freedom of others. Freedom is therefore only possible when one person recognizes the freedom of others. Freedom presupposes a structure of freedom; it requires a social and institutional framework. Law and institutions should not be regarded as the antithesis of freedom, or even primarily as limits on freedom, but as necessary conditions for freedom. Political theology therefore rightly rejects a purely individualistic understanding of reality.

And yet this argument itself reveals an aspect which does not receive its due from the supporters of political theology. Society does not create freedom; on the contrary, it takes for granted that freedom is not under its control, and accepts a responsibility to protect this sovereign freedom at all costs. The freedom of the person, then, does not depend on the favour of society and its institutions, but takes priority over them. It is an essential element of the whole western Christian tradition that the person has a value which is independent of and transcends the social dimension, and we have every reason to fight tooth and nail for this awareness in theory and practice. There is therefore a legitimate area for the private, the intimate and the personal. This means that between person and society, between the area of the personal and the area of the public, there is a permanent tension which cannot be removed. Each needs the other, but neither can be dissolved into the other. Consequently society is not the widest context of reality.

This philosophical argument leads to a theological point. We have just discovered an irreducible tension between the individual person and social reality. This

124 AN INTRODUCTION TO CHRISTIAN FAITH

means that there are alienations both between people
and between the individual and social reality which
are not the result of psychological and sociological
causes and so cannot be eliminated by social action
alone. Human suffering resulting from natural disas-
ters or incurable illness – to take only two examples
– cannot be abolished by social policy. No more is there
a political way to remove the differences and isolation
separating one person from another. There are alienations which are an integral part of the human condition. They are part of the finitude of human nature
and so cannot be removed by human effort. Quite the
reverse, any attempt by a finite human being to take
over the complete control and bring about wholeness
and salvation himself, would inevitably become totalitarian and lead to violence. The desire to control salvation and create it oneself could only lead to the
horror of the worst kind of tyranny. For that reason,
salvation must remain something outside the control
of the individual and of society. The bridging and healing of the split which runs through the whole of reality
can only start from something which encompasses and
unites everything without doing violence to it. This
defines the essence of the absolute. It encompasses
every individual thing and yet releases it into its own
autonomy.

This somewhat abstract discussion can be filled out
by a more down-to-earth argument. The human race
has not in practice been able to withstand the tensions
and polarities I have described. The result has been
violence, injustice and falsehood, which prevent reality from appearing in its unspoilt form. Every human
attempt to create a better and more just order cannot
escape the influence of injustice and falsehood and
must itself turn to violence. All the time we bring the
seed of new unrest and new injustice into the new

order from the beginning. We clearly cannot escape by our own power from the vicious circle of violence and opposing violence, injustice and retribution. There is no purely quantitative solution to the problem of being saved in terms of constantly fresh and greater effort. We need a qualitatively new beginning. That is why the human race, in all its religions and social utopias, has always dreamed of a fundamental transformation of all things and hoped for a completely original new beginning. It is for the sake of society that man in his hope of salvation transcends the dimension of the social. This is the place where it makes sense to talk about redemption and grace and where, for the sake of man, we must speak about them.

I can sum up our conclusion as follows. Human beings do not *have* a need for redemption; their situation is fundamentally, whether they realize it or not, a need for redemption. It is the paradox of human nature that is always infinitely transcending itself, that the meaning of its existence is beyond its reach and to that extent supernatural. Man *is* a natural longing for the supernatural. Only when we reach this dimension have we reached the reality of man and talked about God and his grace in 'secular' terms. In every other case we have practised theological idolatry.

7.3. Grace as the freedom to love

Our debate with political theology has left us with a preliminary, though still very formal, idea of what we mean when we talk about salvation and redemption. Salvation is not something supernatural in the sense that it is, as it were, added to our human nature. Salvation is the freedom of our freedom, its redemption

and liberation to be itself.[8] Salvation is the condition
of the possibility from freedom really to reach its ultimate meaning. Salvation is the new creation which
enables us to have a new history. This may at first
sight seem a surprising statement, but it can be easily
supported by reference to Thomas Aquinas. For him
the supernatural order has not yet become, as it did
for modern scholasticism, an almost independent
realm lying above the natural order. For Aquinas supernatural grace is the instrument by which man can
really attain the ultimate meaning present in germ in
his freedom.[9] These statements are not as abstract as
they sound. They amount to nothing less than an assertion that there is no need for a fundamental opposition between the post-enlightenment idea of
emancipation and the Christian message of redemption. The message of the Gospel is a 'call of freedom'
(Ernst Käsemann); the saving reality of the redemption is the lived reality of freedom.

'Freedom', of course, is a dazzling and much misused
word. This enables us to understand a little why there
has been little talk of freedom in the Church since the
apostle Paul, and why it has largely been left to en-
thusiasts and sectarians. The Church was always ter-
rified of freedom, and so, for the protection of the souls
entrusted to it, was all too ready to take it over in
order to distribute it in minute doses where it seemed
necessary and desirable. Pragmatically, Dostoyevsky's
Grand Inquisitor is quite right when he attacks Jesus:
'For fifteen centuries we've been troubled by this freedom, but now it's over and done with for good.' Theologically, this 'wisdom of experience' is exposed for
what it is by Alyosha Karamazov: 'Your inquisitor
doesn't believe in God – that's all his secret!'[10] To believe in God and to decide that freedom is the ultimate
value in reality is one and the same.

But what is freedom? That freedom is to be distinguished from mere licence was stressed by Hegel. The person who does only what he wants is not free, but unfree; he is abandoned and enslaved to his own caprice. This is also the New Testament's starting-point.[11] The New Testament, however, starts a dimension deeper than political philosophy and theology. The actual area of freedom which a human being needs in order to be free cannot be created exclusively within society. Even the person who is free from all pressures, both internal and external, who can freely control his existence, is far from free in the view of the New Testament. He is not unfree because he does not have sufficient power over himself, but because he wants such power in the first place, because he thinks he can and must take control over himself and his reality. This is an expression of fear and anxiety. Not just this – it is also an expression of an attachment, an addiction, to himself. Such an absence of freedom is the essence of sin. Theologically, sin is not in the first place a moral phenomenon. Sin is when a person is constricted within the narrow limits of his own self, dependent on the familiar and apparently safe, incapable of being free for others and for the unpredictable newness of the future. To sin, in its self-isolating egoism and its obstinate, implacable particularism, which makes self the absolute, its contemporaries and its surroundings must seem a threat, alien and alienating. Its world is no longer possibility and scope, but only a limitation on its freedom, with which it must constantly collide in the struggle for existence, the struggle for power and prestige. Sin is inability to love. That is why it is the opposite of human health and wholeness in and with the world.

Freedom is sparked off only by contact with another freedom. Freedom is possible only through another freedom. Human salvation therefore depends on a person's encountering a free human being. This is what makes an encounter with Jesus Christ a source of salvation. He alone is without sin (Jn 8:46; Heb. 4:15), totally free. He sets himself completely above the tradition of the elders (Mk 7:1–13), and teaches like one who has power (Mk 1:22, 27). In a hitherto unexampled freedom he does not keep to the hallowed ordinances of religion, he associates with the godless, those whom society and religion despise, and yet is sufficiently free to submit to particular ordinances. In man's relations with God, too, the cruel system of guilt and punishment, merit and reward, no longer applies. The householder in Jesus' parable of the labourers in the vineyard pays the same wage to those who did not start until the last hour. When Jesus makes him reply to the complaints of those who had endured the full day's heat, 'Is your eye evil because I am good?' (Mt. 20:15), he is placing himself in opposition to the rigid system of law and substituting the law of grace. This is not a rigid system, but the sovereign freedom of grace. This message, and behaviour which matched it, made Jesus a great disturber of order. Nothing was more natural than that the guardians or order should have wanted to get rid of him as quickly as possible. Order and law required it. Jesus' death on the cross was a final triumph of order, but even more was it a victory for freedom. This is where freedom becomes really free. It lets itself fall into absolute anonymity; it dies in an act of self-sacrifice for the future of those we regard in human terms as having no future. This is where the spell of the individual's attachment to himself and to systems of security is broken. This is where a new possibility appears, a possibility of free existence which accepts history.

What happened in Jesus Christ is so utterly new

that theologians of all periods have had difficulty in understanding it in the categories available to them. This can be shown even of the New Testament writers.[12] To interpret the rôle in salvation of Jesus and his cross they frequently make use of the traditional images of sacrifice, expiation, reparation and representation, and yet they are constantly forced to go beyond the conceptual range of their terms and treat them as mere ciphers of the reality they are in fact discussing. The position is similar with the ideas of the Greek Fathers, who see the salvation brought by Jesus as the overcoming of subjection of death by divinization, or Anselm of Canterbury's satisfaction theory, which became firmly fixed in western theology and treats redemption as the restoration of a great order of justice embracing both God and man. All these interpretations contain many elements of permanently valid human experience and biblical preaching, but they themselves must be interpreted as ways of describing the sovereign freedom of God in his self-giving love, which took particular form in the self-sacrificing freedom of Jesus. Thomas Aquinas followed the road of interpretation to the end. According to Aquinas, Jesus took hold in freedom of the love of God which took hold of him.[13] This obedient love reached its final fulfilment on the cross. Christ's redemptive sacrifice therefore consists in the voluntary sacrifice of his life in obedience to the Father and in the service of man.[14] Through it a new possibility of existence entered the world. For us it is an offer and a challenge, a provocation of love.[15] By accepting this new possibility,[16] we become one with Christ in faith and love, and so share in his life and his freedom.[17] He frees our freedom for service and redeems us for love.

So, by following Thomas Aquinas, we have reached a deeper understanding of redemption and salvation.

'Objective redemption' is not a sort of arsenal of re-
deeming forces subsequently distributed to us in 'subjective redemption'. Even if we want to retain this
misleading terminology, it is Jesus Christ, the new
Adam, who is in person the objective redemption
which frees us for a new human existence by the freedom of love. For us, therefore, the reality of salvation
consists in taking hold in faith of the Gospel of Jesus
Christ, accepting it and living by it. Faith does not
mean just assent to certain truths; in addition, and
more importantly, it is the power given to us by the
love of God which comes to us in Jesus Christ to re-
direct our lives towards God and our fellow men. This
faith, in the sense of admission into Jesus' innermost
attitude to God and other people, is the reality of salvation. It is our reconciliation with ourselves and our
world. By being completely open to God, a believer
shares in God's omnipotence. 'All things are possible
to him who believes' (Mk 9:23). And by becoming effective in love (Gal. 5:6), faith also breaks through the
barriers separating us from other people. So, in faith,
reality starts to become healthy and whole again. This
is the force of the saying, 'Your faith has made you
well' (Mk 10:52; cf. Acts 16:31).

7.4 Christian humour

In the person of Jesus Christ and in his freedom a
fundamental revision of the understanding of existence begins to take shape. Whereas for the Greeks
substance and subsistence, being as such and being in
itself, was the highest and the ultimate, and consequently the highest of all ideas was for them the un-
moved mover which revolved in itself, contemplated
itself and satisfied itself, was loved by all but itself did

not love, now being for others has become the model of freedom. Not self-contained being, but being with others, not self-subsistent being, but going outside oneself, is now true freedom. Love which gives itself, pours itself out, is now the ultimate. It is no less than the definition of God (1 Jn 4:8). The central manifestation of God's sovereign freedom in love is that it can expend itself on man totally, even to death, and still not be exhausted. Powerlessness becomes the model of power; folly becomes the wisdom of God (1 Cor. 7:17-31).

If we want to talk about the revolutionary power of Christianity, this is the right place. Here we have a revolution which goes to the ultimate roots. Anyone who makes it the basis for a revolutionary political programme has understood the fundamental nature of this reversal of all values as little as the person who makes Christianity an ideology of the *status quo*. Both want laws. But Christian faith is characterized not by rigid order and law, not by individual or communal achievement or progress, but by exuberance, extravagance, and freedom from worry and from anxiety. To a society which measures everything by certifiable performance and efficiency this is sheer folly.[18] And yet it is just this which frees us from the inhuman pressure constantly to have to validate oneself to oneself and others by fresh achievement. It sets us free, without making us passive, for an inwardly relaxed, cheerful and truly human human life.

Christian faith produces joy. According to the New Testament, faith is an anticipatory sign of the eschatological reality of salvation. One of the main elements of Christian faith is therefore humour, and the lack of humour and irritability into which we in the contemporary Church and contemporary theology have so often slipped is perhaps one of the most serious objections which can be brought against present-day Christianity. Of course humour is something different from the thin, rarefied, or rather pained, smile of some 'comic saints'. Humour is the attitude which allows man to be totally human and only human because it alone allows God to be God and exposes all other claims to absolute status and honour as ridiculous. 'He who sits in heaven laughs at them' (Ps. 2:5). A correct distinction between God and man is thus the opposite of the deadly seriousness of sin. It is the basis of human wholeness. It makes humour possible. It is a basic form of Christian faith.

Notes

1. J. Kahl, *Das Elend des Christentums oder Plädoyer für eine Humanität ohne Gott* (Hamburg, 1968); cf. the response of J. M. Lohse (ed.), *Menschlich sein – mit oder ohne Gott?* (Stuttgart, 1969).

2. Cf. F. X. Arnold, *Dienst am Glauben: Untersuchungen zur Theologie der Seelsorge,* 1 (Freiburg, 1948); K. Rahner, 'The Word and the Eucharist', *Theological Investigations,* vol. 4 (London & Baltimore, 1966), pp. 253–86; H. Volk, *Zur Theologie des Wort Gottes* (Mainz, 1962); H. Schlier, *Wort Gottes* (Würzburg, 1962); O. Semmelroth, *Wirkendes Wort* (Frankfurt am Main, 1962); L. Scheffczyk, *Von der Heilmacht des Wortes* (Munich, 1966); H. Fries, ed., *Wort und Sakrament* (Munich, 1966).

3. *DS* 1532 = *NR* 722

4. On the connection between alienation and redemption cf. P. Tillich, *'Entfremdung und Versöhnung im modernen Denken',* *WW* IV, pp. 183–199; W. Pannenberg, *What is man? Contemporary anthropology in theological perspective* (Philadelphia, 1970).

5. H. de Lubac, *Surnaturel* (Paris, 1946); *id, The Mystery of the Supernatural* (London, 1967); H. Bouillard, *Conversion et grâce chez S. Thomas d'Aquin* (Paris, 1944); H. Rondet, *Gratia Christi* (Paris, 1948); E. Delaye, 'Ein Weg zur Bestimmung des Verhältnisses von Natur und Gnade', *Orientierung* 14 (1950), pp. 138–41. These ideas were criticized and developed by K. Rahner, 'Concerning the Relationship Between Nature and Grace',

Theological Investigations, vol. 1, pp. 297–317; 'Nature and Grace',
Theological Investigations, vol. 4, pp. 165–88; Hans Urs von Balthasar, *The Theology of Karl Barth* (New York, 1971). The relevant
works of J. Alfaro, J. Ratzinger, H. Volk and others are listed in
Sacramentum Mundi, vol. IV (London, 1969), pp. 180–81.
   6. *DS* 3009; 3015–19; 3033 = *NR* 35; 42–47; 55.
   7. On political theology cf. J. B. Metz, *Theology of the World*
(London & New York, 1969), pp. 107–130; 'Political Theology',
Sacramentum Mundi, vol. V (London, 1970), pp. 34–38; J. Molt-
mann, *Theology of Hope* (London, 1967); *Perspektiven der Theologie*
(Munich & Mainz, 1968); H. Cox, *The Secular City* (London, 1966);
T. Rendtorff & H. E. Tödt, *Theologie der Revolution* (Frankfurt am
Main, 1968); J. B. Metz, J. Moltmann, W. Ölmüller, *Kirche im
Prozess der Aufklärung* (Munich & Mainz, 1970); H. Peukert, ed.,
Diskussion zur politischen Theologie (Munich & Mainz, 1969); H.
Maier, *Kritik der politischen Theologie* (Einsiedeln, 1970); J. Rat-
zinger, *Die Einheit der Nationen. Eine Vision der Kirchenväter*
(Salzburg & Munich, 1971).
   8. On the interpretation of grace as freedom, cf. K. Rahner,
'Freedom in the Church', *Theological Investigations*, vol. 2, pp. 89–
117; *Grace in Freedom* (London, 1969); J. B. Metz, 'Freiheit als
philosophisch-theologisches Grenzproblem', H. Vorgrimler *et al.*,
eds., *Gott in Welt*, vol. 1 (Freiburg, 1964), pp. 287–314; H.
Schürmann, 'Die Freiheitsbotschaft des Paulus – Mitte des Evan-
geliums?', *Catholica* 25 (1971, pp. 22–62
   9. M. Seckler, *Instinkt und Glaubenswille nach Thomas von
Aquin* (Mainz, 1961); *Das Heil in der Geschichte. Geschichtstheo-
logisches Denken bei Thomas von Aquin* (Munich, 1964), esp.
pp. 81–108; E. Schillebeeckx, *The Concept of Truth and Theological Renewal* (London 1968), pp. 30–75; O. H. Pesch, *Theologie der
Rechtfertigung bei Martin Luther und Thomas von Aquin* (Mainz,
1967), pp. 919–35. On Bonaventure's view, in which the theology
of the cross was more important, cf. J. Ratzinger, 'Gratia praesup-
ponat naturam. Erwägungen über Sinn und Grenze eines scholas-
tischen Axioms', J. Ratzinger & H. Fries, eds., *Einsicht und Glaube*
(Freiburg, 1962), pp. 135–49.
   10. F. M. Dostoyevsky, *The Brothers Karamazov* (Harmondsworth 1958), pp. 294, 307.
   11. Cf. H. Schlier, ἐλεύθερος, *TDNT*, vol. II, pp. 497–502;
'Über das vollkommene Gesetz der Freiheit', *Die Zeit der Kirche*
(Freiburg i. Br., 4th ed. 1966), pp. 193–206; R. Bultmann, *Theology
of the New Testament* vol. 1 (London, 1952), pp. 340–52, vol. 2
(London, 1955), pp. 78–79; H. Conzelmann, *Outline of the Theology*

of the New Testament (Munich, 1967); D. Nestle, 'Freiheit', *RAC* VIII (1970), pp. 275–86.
  12. On the role of Jesus' death in salvation, cf. H. Conzelmann, E. Flessmann van Leer, E. Haenchen, E. Käsemann & E. Lohse, *Zur Bedeutung des Todes Jesu. Exegetische Beiträge* (Gütersloh, ²1967); E. Biser, W. Fürst, J. F. G. Göters, W. Kreck & W. Schrage, *Das Kreuz Jesu Christi als Grund des Heils* (Gütersloh, 1967); F. Viering, *Der Kreuzetod Jesu. Interpretation eines theologischen Gutachtens* (Gütersloh, 1969); B. A. Willems, *Erlösung in Kirche und Welt*, Quaestiones Disputatae 35 (Freiburg, 1968); H. Kessler, *Die theologische Bedeutung des Todes Jesu. Eine traditionsgeschichtliche Untersuchung* (Düsseldorf, 1970).
  13. Thomas Aquinas, *Summa theologiae*, III, q. 34, a 3.
  14. *Op. cit.*, q. 48 a 2.
  15. *Op. cit.*, q. 49 a 1.
  16. *Op. cit.*, q. 49 a 3, ad 1.
  17. *Op. cit.*, q. 48 a 2, ad 1.
  18. Cf. H. U. von Balthasar, 'Narrentum und Herrlichkeit', *Herrlichkeit*, vol. III/1 (Einsiedeln, 1965), pp. 492–551; H. Cox, *The Feast of Fools* (Cambridge, Mass., 1969).

8 The ecclesiality of faith

8.1 The Church – an obstacle or an aid to faith?

The title 'the ecclesiality of faith' has a strong tendency to arouse aversion and provoke hostility in many people. It all too readily conjures up ideas of dogmatic spoon-feeding, magisterial baby-minding, thought police and thought control, even of sanctions against dissenters, inquisitions and heresy trials. The Church's claim to have the task of presenting the message of faith authentically and authoritatively, indeed infallibly, seems to be in fundamental contradiction to the modern sense of freedom. The new courage to use one's own intelligence has left Church dogma tainted with dogmatism, and dogmatic intolerance must certainly be regarded today as a danger to society and opposed. Many objections to Christianity concern, not the 'cause' of the faith or the 'cause' of Jesus, but what believers have made of this 'cause'. The real and irremovable scandal of faith, the cross of Jesus Christ, has been obscured by superficial and unnecessary scandals. Here we shouldn't think in the first place of moral scandals, but of the scandal of so many of the Church's structures, which seem to many people obstacles both to human emancipation and happiness and to Christian freedom, and an encouragement to immaturity and authoritarian attitudes.

We must take these objections seriously, even
though they are often put forward with an ideological
intolerance which yields in nothing to the Church's
claim to absoluteness. If the Church claims to be the
normal place where faith becomes credible and the
main reason for its credibility, the endeavour to reform
the Church so as to make it truly evangelical and truly
human is one of the most fundamental elements of its
missionary task, so that the whole appearance of the
Church is a witness to Christ. In this situation it is
not enough to stress and defend against others the
importance of freedom and human dignity, solidarity
and brotherhood; these ideals must also be put into
practice within the community of the Church and in
its structures.

But the questions are much more fundamental. The
real question is, 'Do we need a Church at all? Did
Jesus really intend a Church?' As Loisy put it, he
preached the coming of God's rule and we got the
Church.[1] Doesn't the Church, in its particularity, de-
tract from the universality of Christianity? Shouldn't
we be going outside the Church and trying to imple-
ment Christianity in a secular form? Shouldn't we
replace the dogmas of the Church by a general theory
of Christianity?[2] Such a general theory of Christianity
has a basis in the fact that Christianity, in the course
of its history, has largely shaped the intellectual attitudes and social structures of our predominantly
European and American civilization, and gone on, in
the process of acculturation, to leave its mark on the
whole of world civilization. It was to a large extent
Christianity which made possible the western ideas of
freedom and tolerance, the secular attitude to the
world and the scientific and technical domination of
the world which this made possible. To this extent we
can talk about a structural non-ecclesial Christianity

in our civilization, and say that the boundaries of Christianity are in many respects wider than those of the Church.

Yes but: Christianity without a Church is a utopian fantasy. Christian religious convictions, like all other human beliefs, could not survive for long without some degree of institutionalization.[3] What the institution does, of course, is to set up durable patterns of behaviour and make them habitual. Where this does not happen they usually quickly fade away. Without the challenge of the Churches, which constantly keep alive the memory of the source, of Jesus Christ, a Christianity without a Church wouldn't be likely to survive for more than one or two generations at the most. It is worth reflecting on the fact that Dietrich Bonhoeffer, writing out of his experiences in Nazi Germany, talked about a return to the source which had taken place as a result of the threat of a new barbarism: 'Reason, law, education, humanity, all the lofty ideals, sought and found new meaning and new power in their source'.[4] Of course, the situation of our own society is quite different from that of the Third Reich, though no one would try to maintain that the Christian idea of freedom and humanity is obvious today and needs no institutional protection. Besides, how could Christianity carry on in a world of powerful and over-powerful institutions if it did not become institutionalized? How would the individual Christian carry on believing – we have to put it as strongly as that – if he wasn't carried and supported by the strength of other people's faith? From a sociological point of view, this is the meaning of the Church and the parish: they are not first and foremost large organizations, but are supposed to provide a structure of plausibility for Christian faith.

8.2 The Church as an institution and event

The Church, then, does not exist for its own sake. You can't stand up for it, defend it or love it for its own sake. The Church can only become credible and convincing by virtue of the 'cause' it represents and for the sake of which it exists. Because of this the Church's theological reflection on itself and its structures is, in theological terms, relatively recent. The Church did not become a subject for reflection and official church statements until the late Middle Ages, in response to the conflicts with the emerging nation states, with millenarian movements, with Wycliff and Hus, and above all because of the split in the Church in the West.[5] From the work of the first Vatican Council, and also of the second, there developed almost an ecclesiocentrism which is in marked contrast to the theocentric and Christocentric tradition of the early Church. Many texts of the last council can be criticized for being too much stuck in an immanentist view of the Church, being too often the Church contemplating its own navel, and not talking enough about the 'cause' of the Church. Early Church theology was quite different. Its doctrine of the Church is given classical expression in the Apostles' Creed. Here a distinction is made between faith in God, in Christ, in the Spirit, and the 'I accept the Church' (*credo ecclesiam*).[6] Here the Church is not an object of faith in the same way as God, Jesus Christ and the Spirit. Rather, we take the Church on trust from God. Ecclesiology is therefore included in pneumatology. In this connection the Spirit is not primarily the third divine person, but the power by which the saving action of God in Jesus Christ is present in history. The Church is thus the specific place in which God's saving work in Jesus Christ is made present by the Holy Spirit. Ecclesiology is a function of pneumatology. In modern theology, on the other hand, one often gets the impression that pneumatology has become a function of ecclesiology; the Spirit has become the guarantor of the Church as an institution, and pneumatology has become the ideological superstructure on top of ecclesiology.

Such shifts of emphasis naturally have a visible effect on ecclesiology. An internally based view of the Church will treat the Church more or less as a political and juridical power structure. This is quite possible both in a conservative and a progressive style. The Gospel, salvation and the Spirit become in this view possessions of the Church and are administered by the Church. This results in the Gospel and the Spirit almost being taken under the Church's control, which leaves the Church without any external standard. An ecclesiology of this sort has inoculated itself in advance against any questions. It has become a self-contained system. On the other hand, an ecclesiology built on pneumatology will think of the Church more as an event in which the truth, freedom and justice which entered the world with Christ remain alive in history and are constantly given new life. The Church then exists wherever the 'cause of Jesus' is made present by the Spirit, taken hold of in faith and put into practice in love. In this view the Church is primarily an event; it is something happening.[7]

The Church's being something happening does not exclude institutional forms.[8] Even with the earthly Jesus, the 'cause of Jesus' cannot be separated from his person; indeed it coincides with the evidence of his life, including his death. This inseparability of person and cause, evidence and witness, establishes an important fundamental structure of Christianity. Christian faith is permanently tied to the doctrine delivered once and for all (Jude 3). The authenticity of the Spirit is shown by the fact that he confesses Jesus as the Lord (1 Cor. 12:3), and takes his standards from him. Even in the age of the Church, this permanently binding 'cause of Jesus' cannot be separated from Jesus the witness. This basic law receives classical expression in two passages of Paul. According to 2 Cor.5:18–21 the ministry of reconciliation was instituted in the word and work of reconciliation; both have the same origin. Rom.10:17 sums up this inseparability in the formula *fides ex auditu*. 'How are they to believe in him of whom they have never heard? And how are they to hear without a preacher? And how can men preach unless they are sent?' (Rom.10:14–15). Thus the pneumatological dimension of the Church does not exclude, but includes, commissioning and authority. It is not just human and sociological considerations that give the Church an institutional side, but its theological essence. The Church is always both, institution and event.

However, pneumatology is not only the basis of the institutional aspect; it also limits it. Through the power of the Spirit the Church must again and again break out of the danger of rigidity, must be given new impetus and life. The institutional elements are therefore not guarantees and safeguards for the action of the Spirit. Rather the Church in its visible institution is a sacrament, a reality in sign. Both dogmatic formulas and canonical rules have the character of signs, pointers. Even the historical succession of ministries is not itself the continuity of the Church with its apostolic origin. It is only a sign of the continuity which possesses its reality ultimately only in the Spirit, the Pneuma. Thomas Aquinas considers at one point whether the law of the New Covenant is a written law. His answer to this question is that the law of the New Covenant consists in the grace of the holy Spirit which is given by faith. According to him, therefore, the law of the New Covenant is a law written in our hearts. Written laws have only a secondary role in the New Covenant. Their function is to prepare for the reception of the Spirit and draw the right conclusions about life by the Spirit.[9] This ought to lead on to an extended theological consideration of the relation between institution and event in the Church, but we can only look a little more at one of the many aspects.

8.3 The collective search for truth 'from below'

According to the testimony of Scripture the Spirit has been given to all the baptized.[10] The Spirit is not reserved to a particular class in the Church – we are all spiritual (Gal.6:1). The authority and the mission to bear witness to the 'cause of Jesus' in history is vested primarily in the Church as a whole and all its members. They are all part of a royal nation and holy priesthood with the task of declaring God's wonderful deeds (1 Pet. 2:9; cf. Rev. 1:6; 5:10; 20:6). By baptism all have had the eyes of their hearts enlightened (Eph. 1:18). All have the mind of Christ (1 Cor. 2:16), and sensitivity to discern what is right (Phil. 1:9–10), and so do not need to be taught by anyone (1 Jn 2:20,27).

This fundamental truth of primitive Christianity, that the testimony to the faith had been entrusted to all Christians, was for a long time largely forgotten in the Church. The representative theological dictionary of Wetzer and Welte of 1884 dismisses the entry 'Laity' with the curt remark: 'Laity: see Clergy.' Here the laity were being described as a purely negative entity, as non-clerics. They were laity in the secularized sense of non-specialists who know nothing about the subject and so have no say. It is consequently not surprising that in the same dictionary, under the relevant heading 'Clergy', there appears the terse statement: 'No one can seriously maintain the existence of a priesthood of the laity.' To appeal to the words of 1 Peter in support of this view is said to be 'a sign of great tastelessness and exegetical confusion'. The article will only allow 'a figurative, highly secondary priesthood of believers'.[11]

It is indeed easy to see why Cardinal Newman aroused immense suspicion and hostility when, in 1859, in the atmosphere of this sort of theology, he published his work *On Consulting the Faithful in Matters of Doctrine* and showed that 'the Nicene dogma was maintained during the greater part of the fourth century, not by the unswerving firmness of the Holy See, Councils, or Bishops, but by the "consensus fidelium".'[12] For his evaluation of the *sensus* and *consensus fidelium* Newman could appeal to the Tübingen theologian J. A. Möhler, but his ideas did not have their full effect until our own century. The second Vatican Council states in its Constitution on the Church: 'The body of the faithful as a whole . . . cannot err in matters of belief. Thanks to a supernatural sense of belief which characterizes the People as a whole, it manifests this unerring quality when, "from the bishops down to the last member of the laity", it shows universal agreement in matters of faith and morals' (12). This statement must be seen in conjunction with the statement in the Constitution on Revelation that the Church transmits her faith, not just in dogmatic formulas, but through 'all that she herself is, all that she believes' (8). Thus the laity's experience and practice of the faith forms part of the Church's testimony to the faith.

If differences arise between the official doctrinal teaching of the Church and the laity's everyday experience of the faith – as is often the case today –

these conflicts cannot be resolved simply by a repetition and tightening up of the traditional dogmatic formulas without discussion. The truth of the Gospel can only emerge from a consensus. An attitude of obedience to ecclesiastical authority is not the principal expression of the ecclesiality of faith. Membership of the Church is not demonstrated by blind obedience, but by listening to others and being willing to accommodate them. Each person is supposed to support the others in the faith, stimulate them and, if necessary, also criticize them. Scripture says that each person has his or her gift (1 Cor. 7:7; 1 Pet. 4:10). All must listen to each other and learn from each other: the teachers must listen to the pastors, the pastors to the teachers and prophets, and they in turn model themselves on those who have the gift of really ministering in the Church. In other words, obedience in the Church can never be described as a one-way process; it is an interaction.

8.4. Three criteria

It is at this point, in the Church as it is, that practical difficulties appear. In the past it was relatively easy to achieve a fair degree of unity and unanimity in the Catholic faith. The overwhelming majority of Catholics lived in a homogeneous environment which was practically permeated with Catholic attitudes. And while, even in the past, different theological schools and types of piety existed, and were even institutionalized in the orders, this was all within a common conceptual framework; it was possible to identify and understand the other person's position and possible to say where and why one disagreed with him. Today, in contrast, intellectual assumptions have become so dif-

ferent, and the range of problems so great, that discussion in the Church has become enormously
difficult. It is no longer possible for someone to know
all the positions, let alone give an adequate assess-
ment of them. This has resulted in a new sort of pluralism.[13] The question is how the Church's unity in
faith can still be made visible in these circumstances.
Hasn't this process already made the Church's testimony unclear? Hasn't it lost its unequivocalness and
clarity? How, in these circumstances, can the Church
still be a city built on a mountain-top, a light placed
on a candle-stick? It is a worrying question. One answer, however, is ruled out, and that is a return to a
position based solely on doctrinal authority. Not only
is it theologically indefensible, because it contradicts
the truth that all have a mission and a responsibility,
but it could also not be successful, at least in the long
term. It wouldn't be long before it proved a Pyrrhic
victory. Once questions have emerged, it may be possible to suppress them temporarily, but they will not
go away for good. This means that any conservative
or traditionalist movement must also argue its case,
and all argument inevitably provokes new questions.
So the problem is: how can the Christian faith preserve
its uniquivocalness and its unity at least in fundamentals. How in practical terms can the ecclesial dimension of faith be preserved today?

The text from the Constitution on the Church to
which I have already referred (12) suggests three criteria. The first is the Holy Spirit. To a purely legalistic
and dogmatic attitude this may sound surprising. In
the council documents, however there is nothing unusual about this statement. In the Constitution on the
Church, the Church is said to include all who possess
the Holy Spirit (14). Membership of the Church and
correct beliefs within the Church ultimately escapes

legal formulation and dogmatic definition. Unity in faith can be achieved neither by uniform dogmatic formulae nor by democratic majority decisions. What we are dealing with is a system of knowledge which differs both from authoritarian and from democratic processes of decision. Consensus in faith and the determination of a consensus is a spiritual process. It can only be detected by the *sensus fidei* produced by the Spirit, an interior feel, a sort of sixth sense for faith. We could put it another way and say that dogmatic statements only make sense when you stay inside the language-game of faith. In purely intellectual terms you can go on discussing and making distinctions for ever. You can go on interpreting until the boundaries between faith and unbelief, orthodoxy and heresy, are hopelessly blurred. Often a purely intellectual process will not produce agreement or clarity about where truth ends and error begins. Nevertheless the Church must make unequivocal statements at least on fundamentals. This is only possible by spiritual judgment. The only way to be sure of the shared truth in the faith is by doing the truth together. This may, or rather must, show whether people belong together or have in fact grown apart.

To prevent such a spiritual judgment from being purely arbitrary or leading to untenable and insubstantial enthusiasm, the Constitution on the Church specifies a second criterion. It says that the sense of the faith must be related to the prior content of the faith as it was delivered once and for all (Jude 3). Since the Spirit is the Spirit of Christ, he must remind us of the words and works of Christ (cf. Jn 14:26; 16:13–14). The faith of the Church is therefore not just a projection and objectivation of subjective states of religious feeling; it must develop and define itself in an encounter with the objective testimonies to the faith contained in Scripture and tradition. The Church possesses a standard which is prior to it and imposes a duty on it. It is not superior to, but subordinate to, the word of revelation. In everything it says and does it must demonstrate its fidelity to revelation. In other words, it must argue. For the creation of a 'rational' and responsible consensus, therefore, there is a need for religious and theological information, especially adult education in theology, or adult catechesis. In this context the confrontation with Scripture and tradition can possess a power which is critical and liberating. It can prevent the Church's faith from being trapped by the *sensus communis*, the commonplaces of a particular period's intellectual fancy or fashion uncritically and without any outside criteria, or from becoming a prisoner of its own pet ideas.

There is a growing unwillingness, even an inability, to think historically and to expose oneself to criticism from historical sources; this is affecting the Church and theology, and it is dangerous. It is also possible to be swept off one's feet by critical ideas. Criticism which begins to shrink from critical examination turns into hypocrisy and degenerates into ideological self-righteousness.

8.5. Authority in the Church

The Gospel's permanent normative and critical function as the standard of the Church and its faith is also expressed in the third criterion listed by the Constitution on the Church in its definition of the ecclesiality of faith: union with authority in the Church. It is no accident that the magisterium is only mentioned in third place. The ecclesiality of faith is not exhausted by an attitude of obedience to the Church's teaching authority. That authority is situated within the community of believers and under the authority of the word of revelation.[14] It is not a super-criterion ruling over the Church and its common search for truth in lonely Olympian majesty and issuing condemnations. The magisterium is rather responsible for the emergence of the right relation between the community of believers and the content of faith which is prior to it, and it is responsible for ensuring proper communication within the Church. It can therefore be described as service in two ways, service to the word and service to the community.

Authority in the Church is in the service of the word of the Gospel. It is responsible for seeing that the Church takes its position from the authority of the Gospel, and not from other authorities. In other words, authority represents the way the Gospel is external to the Church. To the extent that it symbolically represents and gives effect to the priority and otherness of the Gospel, it is itself external to the community. To put it in other terms, the magisterium can only represent the Church by representing the external element in terms of which alone the Church can regard itself as the Church. But this also means that the authority of the magisterium is none other than the authority of the Gospel which it serves. To that extent, while its service excludes power, it includes authority. Power is being able to force one's will on others, whereas authority sets the other person free to enjoy his or her own freedom; it does not make him a slave but a master. Christian freedom is, as we know, a freedom set free by the Gospel (Gal. 5:1). It would make a great difference if the magisterium were to make its connection with the Gospel clear in institutional terms, and if it were to demonstrate its rôle of service in principle and in practice. This could make an enormous contribution to settling the crisis of authority.

Service of the Gospel is also service of the community. Authority is meant to make the community free and capable of performing its own service (cf. Eph. 4:12). It would be a rather naive faith in harmony to rely entirely on the interchange of different views to bring the Church's sense of faith gradually into a rational mean, and to hope that in the end truth would prevail by virtue of better arguments. That is an ideal but unfortunately not reality. Such an ideal presupposes that an open dialogue exists in the Church in which everyone is willing to listen to other people and to be persuaded by them, and in which there are no such things as vested interests, arrogance and obstinacy. Since this is clearly not so, the area of communication and dialogue must constantly be kept open. Institutionalized authority is – or is meant to be – something like institutionalized freedom. It ought to be a centre of communication, responsible for seeing that everyone has a say. In this general dialogue it ought to articulate and emphasize shared basic convictions, but too often it is prevented from doing so by its own isolation and inability to communicate. Today in the Church we suffer, not from an excess of authority, but from a lack of genuine authority which is in a position to articulate the faith that is binding on all in such a way that all people of good will can see themselves represented in it and a consensus is created. Unfortunately authority has largely lost this mediating function because it has become a faction within the Church. This has brought it into a conflict of rôles from which it has not yet found a way out.

My view of authority, then, is fundamentally that it is one service among other services and depends on contact and communication with the other services.

Now it is Catholic teaching that authority can also take decisions alone and give a final ruling.[15] In traditional theology this is described as the extraordinary form of the exercise of the magisterium. In the language of modern constitutional law it could be called an emergency power. There can be situations in the Church in which, for some reason, the normal forms of communication do not function, but in which the survival of the Church requires a clear statement and decision. Then authority has the right and duty to give a lead in witnessing to the faith and to act as the voice of the Church's faith. In such a situation the magisterium does not speak in its own name, but acts as representative of the Church's faith; it then enjoys an infallibility which is an attribute of the whole Church.[16] Such an extraordinary decision can therefore have only one purpose, namely to restore the normal forms of collective discovery of the truth. No sensible authority would want to govern indefinitely with emergency powers, but in practice in the Church we live with a permanent suspension of the constitution. In the normal situation the magisterium should therefore adhere to the proper forms for collective and collegial (conciliar and synodal) discovery of the truth. This could only benefit its authority in a crisis. Otherwise the sword could easily be found blunt when it was really needed.

8.6. A new form of ecclesiality: orthodoxy through dialogue

After stating and explaining the three criteria, I am now in a position to sketch at least in outline a new form of ecclesial orthodoxy. Two possibilities have been ruled out, a monolithic Church unity guaranteed

by authority, and disintegration into a totally incom-
municable liberal pluralism, and the only alternative
is orthodoxy regarded as a process based on dialogue.
This approach is based on the conviction that truth in
the Church has to emerge from a process of dialogue
between all the charisms and tendencies. A person is
orthodox and a member of the Church as long as he or
she is prepared to preserve the connection of dialogue
with the ecclesial community, as long as he or she
allows its statements a binding claim, accepts them as
a challenge to which he or she gives full weight in
relation to his or her own subjective religious convictions. It is possible to take such a position honourably
even if one is unable at a particular moment to identify
with all the dogmatic statements the Church has made
in the course of almost two millennia, indeed if one is
unable to work up much interest in them at all. We
would all indeed be hopelessly overtaxed in our faith
if we tried to internalize all the truths of faith the
Church has defined in the same way. A merely partial
identification can be quite legitimate, and is not to be
dismissed as a fringe Christianity.

A concept of orthodoxy as based on dialogue does
not exclude the drawing of clear boundaries. One position which is excluded is that which just has no more
time for the Church's teaching and totally refuses to
recognize it as a possibility in terms of the Gospel.
Also excluded is the sort of wild radicalism which
proclaims its own intellectual honesty and throws out
formulae which allegedly make no sense to what it
calls modern religious feeling. Intellectual honesty includes awareness of the limitations of one's own position and the courage to let others change your mind.
Someone who can no longer accept this has already
excluded himself from the community of believers, and
it is merely an act of honesty and respect, both for his

own convictions and those of others, when the Church
also acknowledges this difference. However, sanctions
of this sort should be limited to such clear and fundamental issues as are mentioned in Scripture. For
example, when Paul pronounces an anathema against
anyone who preaches a different gospel (Gal. 1:6), he
is not concerned with just any dogmatic issues, but
with the central element of his Gospel message, that
salvation comes only from the cross of Christ. The
same applies to 1 John. Its condemnation is directed
at those who deny that Jesus is the Christ (1:22; 5:1),
the Son of God (4:15, 5:5), who has come in the flesh
(4:2). A Church which could no longer speak with one
voice on these matters would already have given up.

An act of formal declaration that a position is incom-
patible with the Church's teaching is still possible in
the future, particularly where basic convictions about
the faith are involved, and may, in some circumstances, even be necessary. However it is significant
that the second Vatican Council pronounced no such
anathema, although it proclaimed truths of much
more fundamental significance than, say, the last two
Marian dogmas. Indeed the council even went a step
further. It partially and in practice lifted the anathema pronounced by the first Vatican Council against
those who did not believe in the primacy and infallibility of the pope. This came about in its admission of
Orthodox Christians to the eucharist in certain circumstances.[17] Eucharistic community is ecclesial community. This is a first faint glimmer of the possibility
that the Church may, while continuing to maintain as
true a truth it has once defined, withdraw the anathema associated with it. This could have important
consequences for ecumenical dialogue. Who would
then say that every truth of faith which one maintains
absolutely oneself requires a breaking of ecclesial com-

munity with everyone else who has a different opinion on this matter, even though one may agree with them in the fundamental and central Christian affirmations?

In conclusion, let a remark of the great Tübingen theologian J. A. Möhler sum up what we have been saying. Möhler says that there are two extremes in the life of the Church and both are essentially egoism. In the first everyone wants to be everything; that is extreme ecclesial individualism. In the second one person wants to be everything; that is extreme ecclesial centralism. 'In the first case everything disintegrates to such an extent and it becomes so cold around the Church that people freeze. In the second the bond of unity becomes so tight and love so warm that it is no longer possible to avoid suffocation. We do not want either to freeze in extreme individualism or to suffocate in extreme centralism. That is only possible when both extremes are avoided.' 'Neither one person nor everyone must try to be everything; only all together can be everything, and only a whole can be the unity of all. That is the idea of the Catholic Church.'[18]

Notes

1. A. Loisy, *L'Evangile et l'Eglise* (Paris, 1902), p. 111.
2. As argued principally by T. Rendtorff, following R. Rothe; see Rendtorff's *Kirche und Theologie. Die systematische Funktion des Kirchenbegriffs in der neueren Theologie* (Gütersloh, 1966); J. Matthes, *Religion und Gesellschaft. Einführung in die Religionssoziologie*, vol. I (Hamburg, 1967); *Kirche und Gesellschaft. Einführung in die Religionssoziologie*, vol. II (Hamburg, 1969); W. D. Marsch, *Institution im Übergang. Evangelische Kirche zwischen Tradition und Reform* (Göttingen, 1970).
3. On the concept of an institution cf. H. Dombois, ed., *Recht und Institution* (Witten, 1956); H. Schelsky, 'Ist Dauerreflexion institutionalisierbar? Zum Thema einer modernen Religionsso-

ziologie', *Auf der Suche nach der Wirklichkeit* (Düsseldorf & Cologne, 1965), pp. 250–75; P. L. Berger & T. Luckmann, *The Social Construction of Reality* (London, 1969); H. Schelsky (ed.), *Zur Theorie der Institution* (Düsseldorf, 1970).

4. D. Bonhoeffer, *Ethik* (Munich, 1949), p. 60.

5. Cf. Y. Congar, 'Die Lehre von der Kirche', *Handbuch der Dogmengeschichte*, vol. III/3c and 3d (Freiburg, 1971).

6. Cf. above Chapter 6, notes 4 and 8.

7. Cf. H. Fries, *Kirche als Ereignis* (Düsseldorf, 1958).

8. On the relation between institution and charism the discussion between R. Sohm and A. von Harnack is still relevant: cf. R. Sohm, *Kirchenrecht*, vol. I (Munich & Leipzig, 1892); *Wesen und Ursprung des Katholizismus* (Leipzig & Berlin, ²1912, reprinted Darmstadt, 1967); A. von Harnack, *The Constitution and Law of the Church in the First Two Centuries* (London, 1910); K. Holl, 'Der Kirchenbegriff des Paulus im Verhältnis zu dem der Urgemeinde', *Gesammelte Aufsätze* vol. II (Tübingen, 1928), pp. 920–47; J. L. Leuba, *Institution und Ereignis. Gemeinsamkeiten und Unterschiede der Beiden Arten von Gottes Wirken nach dem Neuen Testament* (Göttingen, 1957); R. Bultmann, *Theology of the New Testament* vol. 2 (London, 1955), pp. 95–100; E. Käsemann, 'Sentences of Holy Law in the New Testament' *New Testament Questions of Today* (London, 1969), pp. 66–81; H. Conzelmann, *Outline of the Theology of the New Testament* (London, 1969); H. Dombois, *Das Recht der Gnade. Ökumenisches Kirchenrecht*, vol. I (Witten, ²1969); G. Hasenhüttl, *Charisma – Ordnungsprinzip der Kirche* (Freiburg, 1969).

9. Thomas Aquinas, *Summa theologiae* I/II, q. 106, a 2.

10. F. X. Arnold, 'Kirche und Laientum', *Glaubenverkündigung und Glaubensgemeinschaft* (Düsseldorf, 1965); Y. Congar, *Lay People in the Church* (London, 1965); H. Küng, *The Church* (London & New York, 1968),pp. 370–87.

11. *Kirchenlexikon*, vol. VII (1891), p. 1323, s.v. 'Laien'; vol. III (1884), p. 546, s.v. 'Clerus'.

12. J. H. Newman, *On Consulting the Faithful in Matters of Doctrine* (London, 1961), p. 77

13. See above, Chapter 1, note 2.

14. *Dogmatic Constitution on Divine Revelation (Dei Verbum)* 10.

15. *DS* 3065–75 = *NR* 384–388. On the interpretation of the First Vatican Council, cf. the essays in *De doctrina Concilii Vaticani primi* (Vatican City, 1969).

16. *DS* 3074 = *NR* 388.

17. Decree on Ecumenism, *Unitatis Redintegratio*, 15.

18. The remark comes from a recollection of Brentano's reported to me by P. B. Gams; cf, J. R. Geiselmann's commentary on Möhler's *Symbolik* (Darmstadt, 1961), p. 698.

9 The historical nature of faith

9.1 History – our biggest problem

At the beginning of this century Ernst Troeltsch, the Protestant theologian and historian of religion, stated his belief that the encounter between theology and history would in the future raise far greater problems than the encounter between theology and natural science which was the main intellectual excitement of his day.[1] In the subsequent period Troeltsch's predictions have been fully realized. History is today our biggest problem.[2] We are currently experiencing a radical 'historicalization' of all areas of reality. Everything is involved in upheaval and change; hardly anything fixed or solid is left. Not even the Church and its understanding of the faith have escaped this historical transformation. To many the Church, the magisterium and dogmas appeared as the solid tower in the surge of time, the immovable rock amid the waves of history. Many felt that here they had a firm anchor in the flux of time and the swift flow of historical attitudes and ideologies. Many serious Christians are now finding, with anxiety, that even in the Church everything has been thrown open for discussion, that the views and positions for which they were yesterday required to do battle, and for which they let themselves be attacked out of loyalty to the Church, are now allegedly or in fact being abandoned by that very Church. The Church's most faithful adherents and the most zealous defenders of the faith see themselves as a result abandoned by the very stewards of the magisterium. Troeltsch was right: everything is shaking.

In the Church and in matters of faith this upheaval in general attitudes is particularly violent, and for many people disturbing. The reason is that the Church and its basic creeds acquired their form in the ancient world. Ancient thought was based on the idea of a cosmos with eternal laws of being. Naturally there was movement and change even here, but these were regarded as something like phenomena on the surface of an eternal ground of being, accidental changes to a permanent substance. The phenomenon of history and historical change was never explicitly discussed. History was a phenomenon within the framework of an encompassing order. In contrast, for modern thought history is not a moment in an encompassing order; on the contrary, every order is a moment within a history which the next instant makes it relative. In this view reality does not have a history; it is itself history through and through.

The great shift to a historical outlook,[3] for which the foundations had been laid by humanism, took place around the beginning of the nineteenth century. In art and philosophy this revolution took the form of the romantic movement and German idealism. For Hegel truth is the whole. 'But the whole is nothing other than essence consummating itself through its development.' 'The True is thus the Bacchanalian revel in which no member is not drunk.'[4] What is said in idealist philosophy of the absolute spirit is said in existentialist philosophy of man. Man does not just live in a history which remains in some way external to him; on the contrary history is the inner dimension and make-up of man. Man is the being who is moving between being and becoming, past and present. In the crucial situations of his life man is constantly at stake; he is profoundly historical. By now we have got tired again of the existentialist jargon of historicality; instead we want to put the emphasis back on real history. Often people draw on Marx and neo-Marxism and say that man's task is to transform the world historically by his labour, through technology and civilization, to make it into a human world, in which he can live and support himself. In other words, the world is not finished, but involved in a continuous process in which man and the world mutually change and affect each other. It is not an eternal natural order, but an historical world.

Remarkably, the growth of historical awareness in the course of the modern period is based on a break with previous history. History could not be experienced as history until historical tradition was no longer an automatically lived reality, but was felt as a past which had been surmounted, which people were striving critically to get beyond. To this extent the emergence of historical awareness is based on the modern swing to subjectivity. This meant a relativization of the previous argument from authority, and presented a fundamental challenge to the absolute validity of sacred documents. In this way it made possible and legitimized a completely new relation to history and a critically distanced confrontation with tradition. The practical consequences of this revolution in awareness can hardly be overestimated. The humanist Laurentius Valla's demonstration of the inauthenticity of the Constantinian Donation meant an unprecedented shaking of the authority and power of the papacy, and Christianity has even now not completely digested the publication by Lessing of the Wolfenbüttel Fragments, with their denial of the resurrection of Christ. The questions of exegesis and the history of doctrine raised by men like Richard Simon, Solomon Semler and later Baur and D. F. Strauss, still continue to occupy theology down to today. Not the least of the merits of the Catholic Tübingen School of the last century was that it was already courageously facing these questions in its day and so inaugurated a new form of theology.

Some of the groups of questions thrown up by historical scholarship can be mentioned at least in broad outline. Comparative religion and exegesis have demonstrated the historical conditioning of the biblical message, its dependence on other religions, on literary genres, conceptual, linguistic and imaginative forms of its time, its historical development and the resulting tensions between individual biblical statements. The results of sociological and historical study have revealed many outward forms and structural elements of the Church as temporally conditioned, and the corresponding doctrines as suspect of ideology, that is, of being a super-structure and canonization of a particular historical and sociological *status quo*. The upheaval is most striking in moral theology.[5] A change in moral awareness and accepted human standards is not just something which can be detected in the past; in the present conflict of generations it is almost tangible. There is a history of human freedom in which we have been constantly discovering more and more the value of personal conscience. This is a further sign of the increasing awareness of human historicality.

It will be seen that the problem of historicality within theology is not restricted to a few issues in exegesis, and dogmatic and moral theology. It is universal, and affects modern thought and faith totally. It presents a radical challenge to Christianity's claim to absoluteness. We must therefore ask very seriously how this radically historical outlook is to be judged theologically. Does it destroy any security in faith and lead to a theological relativism in which anything is valid and so nothing is valid any more? Or does it mean a new opportunity for a deeper understanding of the faith? One's theological attitude to modern thought largely depends on the answers given to these questions.

9.2 Christian faith under the law and promise of history

We start with one of the most fundamental distinctions between the revelation of the Old and New Testament on the one hand and the mythologies and nature religions of the ancient world on the other: Christian faith is completely and utterly a historical religion. Whereas it can be said of the myths that they are always happening and never happened (Sallust), the fundamental confession of the Christian faith is 'Jesus is the Lord' (1 Cor.12:3). God's relinquishing of himself into history in Jesus Christ is nothing other than the conclusion of a long historical dialogue conducted by God at various times and in many ways through the prophets (cf. Heb.1:1). Not nature and not the depths of the human soul, but history, is the dimension in which as Christians we encounter God. The task of Christian faith is therefore not to teach people about an anonymous ultimate basis of reality, nor even about the God of the philosophers, a superior and supreme being, but to bear witness to the God of Abraham, Isaac and Jacob (Pascal). Its task is not to represent a system of abstract truths or a general world view, but to proclaim the mighty historical deeds of God and make them present in word and sacrament.

The fact that Christian faith, because of its object, is historical faith means that we cannot avoid the problems with which history confronts us today by withdrawing to a postulated inner sphere of faith and dismissing historical questions as irrelevant to faith. Such an escape from history is attempted today in two ways. Either you make the Church's faith an ultimate, which carries its own guarantee and cocoons you away from all questions, even if the historical problems tower all around (the Catholic danger), or you attempt to interpret the faith existentially and escape into an area of calm through a more or less empty credulity. This is to make the individual venture of faith an ultimate, no longer related to a specific historical identity, but only to the mere affirmation of the coming of Jesus. The meaning of history is then fulfilled in the presence of faith.[6] In both cases faith is not vulnerable to history because fundamentally history no longer has any meaning for it. In both cases the relation to history which constitutes the Christian faith is denied, and the essence of Christian faith is called in question. Those who think in this way succumb to a new form of docetism; they turn the incarnation into an appearance and faith into a new myth. But if faith rejects history in this way, must not history reject faith? Today above all, we have every reason to stress the historical character of Christianity and to say that God has really entered this ordinary history of ours, adopted it and redeemed it. A onesided ecclesial or existential interpretation of faith makes Christianity atemporal and exalts God above history.

In spite of these criticisms we should be wrong to ignore the relative truth and legitimate concern of existentialist theology. This leads us to a second aspect. It is true that faith does not consist just in assent to the truth of objective facts of salvation. God's action in history is never simply one fact among others; it cannot, like the others, be neutrally observed and checked. For human eyes God's action is hidden action; it is always incognito and cannot be recognized by analogy with other historical events. God's action can only be perceived as such in faith. Only the person who is prepared in faith to break out of the world of the measurable and calculable, out of his comfortable and automatic habits, and entrust himself to the newness of the world of faith, can recognize God's salvation in history. A human being's total openness and self-surrender are the empty mould which is filled by God, who is always greater, and his self-surrender to history. Only where God's action in history is accepted as such, recognized, in human faith and so reaches its goal, only there does it produce salvation, only there does history become salvation history. Salvation history is thus not history without human beings; salvation history only comes into being in God's historical dialogue with human beings. It is not a history which rolls on indifferently, which overtakes human beings almost deterministically; it happens through the historical venture of faith. It is history which happens (M. Buber).

We cannot therefore be content just to stress the objective character of salvation history, important though this is to rebut subjectivist tendencies to minimize it. A pure objectivisim which denied the subjective historicality of faith would be just as one-sided and just as deadly. This subjective historical aspect is of considerable importance for many matters connected with the relationship between faith and history. It is even crucial in the consideration of the miracles, of the resurrection of Jesus and of the historical reliability of the biblical accounts in general. True though it is that faith has to do with a history which confronts it, it is also true that it is impossible to retreat behind faith to facts which give faith security. The certainty of faith can only be obtained through the medium of a historical venture.

In the single reality of Christianity we must thus hold on to two aspects: the word which is uttered in history and the answer which is uttered in history. Christianity reveals itself to us as an historical dialogue between God and man; it takes place in principle wherever human beings trust themselves to the transcendence which opens to them in their freedom. But this dialogue between God and human beings can be disrupted; word and answer can fail to match. God's historical call can die away unheard, and become judgment instead of salvation. This leads us to a third aspect, the distinction between secular history and salvation history. This distinction is extremely problematic. It is impossible to make a clear distinction betwen secular history and salvation. History cannot be divided into two halves, a light side and a dark side. All reality is dominated by the appeal and offer of God's grace and so is potentially salvation history. That is why there are holy pagans and pagan prophets.[7] The reason why a distinction is still made between salvation history in the broad sense and salvation history in the narrow sense is that, as Christians, we start from the premiss, that in the history of Israel, which was fulfilled and transcended in Jesus of Nazareth, the word of God reached its goal 'infallibly', was received 'pure' and attested 'correctly', that here God's dialogue with man 'succeeded' and that this gives us a standard by which to judge all other history.

Naturally not even salvation history 'succeeds' at one go. It has a history of its own, which it needs to realize its identity. We should therefore not be surprised to find mythological, polytheistic and pagan elements persisting in the Old Testament, at odds both with the New Testament and with our rational outlook. Nor does the New Testament succeed everywhere to the same extent in capturing the reality and truth of Jesus Christ. Salvation history must therefore be taken as a whole; we must look at its overall testimony and overall movement. That is the meaning of the hermeneutical principle of the *analogia fidei*. The point of reference for all of salvation history is Jesus Christ. In him the history of God with human beings has 'succeeded' definitively. All scriptural statements must be interpreted critically as directed towards him or based on him. In him something definitive took place which has the power to give all the rest of history proportion and solidity.

But to say that Jesus Christ is the definitive beginning also means that with him salvation has not yet reached its goal in every respect and that the fulfilment of this beginning still lies ahead. The Church is therefore placed between the already and the not yet. It is permanently tied to the 'beginning in fulness' (J. A. Möhler) and dependent on tradition. However, this tradition is no fixed collection of *dicta probantia*, but a living process. As an eschatological phenomenon the Church must again and again go beyond itself and enter afresh into its own future; the proclamation of its own transitoriness is what it lives by (Karl Rahner). The Church does not possess the truth in any simple way, but must keep on looking for it afresh. This takes place in its patient and courageous attention to the 'signs of the time'. The second Vatican Council's *Pastoral Constitution on the Church in the Modern World* carefully spelt out this inescapable temporal coefficient of preaching by saying on the one hand that the Church's proclamation of the Gospel must always give an answer to the questions of the day, while also being well aware that the Church does not have this answer pat. As the Council saw, the questions of the day require a new and deeper exploration of the Gospel and so stimulate new answers which are not just an abstract conclusion from past beliefs. To find this answer the Church and its preaching and theology must often take the path of historical experiment and risk, since just to say the same thing in different situations one has to say it differently each time.

And so we must say that the Church is an historical Church and a pilgrim Church, a searching, struggling, battling Church, a Church of saints and of sinners. It bears the form of history and is bound by the law of history. It must again and again be led by the holy Spirit into all truth (cf. Jn 16:13). That is why there is not only a history of the Church and a history of theology, but also a history of dogma and a history of faith.[9] In this history there takes place not just an ever deeper penetration into truth and an organic growth of biblical seeds into ever taller and thicker trees of dogmatic systems. In the history of dogma there is also a history of forgetting, of inability and failure. Like all history, it is a constant up and down of great periods and ages in danger of getting lost in superficialities and trivia. Consequently the word of the Church is not simply and in every respect the word of God; the Church is only always starting out again in search of it. It must always give the answer of faith in obedience historically, in a new way, and in the process daily confess its guilt, its failure to reach its goal.

In the historical journey of the Church, the return of the whole of history to God is taking place in its beginnings. This directs our attention to a final point. This is the fact that the history of God with human beings is not a particular history alongside other history. No, the whole reality of creation from the very beginning was created for Christ (Col. 1:16, Eph. 1:10) and related to salvation history. Even the reality of creation is therefore determined through and through by history.[10] History is the ultimate framework of all reality.

The things that happen in history are theologically not mere stirrings on the surface of an eternal ground of being, not a fleeting shadow of the eternal, but the real 'nature' of things themselves. There is no metaphysical structure of order to be disentangled from all the detail of history and salvation history. Theologically there is only one permanent fact, that man has been called by God in history and asked for an answer. The effect of this historical word demanding an answer is his 'nature'; it is the source of his constantly unique dignity. His task is to realize that nature and dignity in constantly new ways in historical obedience and responsibility to God.

Christian behaviour in the world should therefore be marked by a boldness towards history. A Christian should be involved with whatever is new; his task is to venture into the untried and unforeseeable and not to cling conservatively to the *status quo* or instinctively long for what is past. In the face of all fainthearted immobility the Christian should be a sign of hope in this timid world so preoccupied with security. If it is true that God is the youngest of us all, then a Christian must remain always young and supple, recognize the 'signs of the times', and respond to them in faith.

To sum up, we may say that history and historicality are basic categories of Christian faith. The Christian faith is historical in its content, its performance, its transmission and its total perspective. It can even be said that the category of history was first discovered within biblical faith. The historical attitude of recent centuries owes something to the historical faith of the Bible; it is something like a secularized version of it. For this reason the modern historical attitude need not necessarily be a challenge to faith and theology. It can also be a welcome new opportunity to perceive and formulate the core of the message of faith better and more appropriately. It must not be seen just as a threat; it must primarily be regarded as a *kairos* for the Church. But on the other side the historical attitude does seem today to be attacking Christian faith; it seems to be emptying it of content and making it relative. Christianity even seems to be abolishing itself in modern historical thinking. To try to deal to some extent with this dichotomy we must look for the permanent element in history, and try to reach a clear distinction between historicality and an all-devouring relativism.

9.3. The permanent element in Christianity

The search for the permanent element in history is not just a theological problem. Meaningful human existence is only possible if something exists which endures, which has validity and permanence. Otherwise such basic forms of human behaviour as trust and loyalty would no longer be conceivable. The only attitude then would be 'Let us eat and drink, for tomorrow we die' (1 Cor. 15:32). There is thus no theological short-cut to a solution of our problem; we must work through a philosophical reflection on what is meant by the words 'history' and 'historicality'.

'History' and 'historicality' have become vogue words in present-day philosophical and theological language. For some people they and what they stand for have something almost frightening about them. They confuse them with relativism, indifferentism and instability in general. For others the word 'historical' has already become almost a new creed and a token of their own progressiveness. As a result the words are charged with all possible emotions and animosities. We have to ask therefore what they really mean.

It is important that history is not confused with the neutral temporal phenomenon of the before and after of motion (Aristotle), the mere succession of years, days and hours, the constant up and down of coming to be and passing away to which all finite things are subject. Aristotle, and still more clearly Augustine, knew that this before and after exists only in relation to the human mind which transcends the before, which no longer is, and the after, which is not yet, by remembering the one and anticipating the other in hope or fear.[11] It derives this power of making things present from its freedom, which is not tied to the peg of the moment (Nietzsche), but transcends every given and can therefore combine past, present and future and imagine them together. History therefore exists only where there is freedom. It is only through freedom that time solidifies into history. For the same reason history must not be identified with organic development. History does not unfold, but is always at stake anew in choice.

But the issue in human freedom is not just this or that, but the whole, the unconditioned; what is decided here is the meaning of man and his world. In freedom man is confronted with a claim which affects him unconditionally (Tillich). Freedom can therefore not be content with a mere up and down, a constant coming to be and passing away. Just because of its universal openness freedom demands specific decision. It is in his very unconditional attachment that man becomes free from subjection to the moment; it is by freeing himself from the slavery to the aimless wandering of instincts that he becomes free for goals he has freely chosen. That is why a bachelor freedom which always wants to be untrammelled and never tied down is not the highest form of freedom, but its ridiculous and squandered caricature. We may therefore define freedom as the capacity for definitiveness. This means that not only the changeable and transitory, but also the unconditioned and definitive, are part of the essence of history. Anyone therefore who uses the historicality of human beings as a pretext for avoiding any statements or decisions which imply definitiveness should consider what he is saying or doing.

Nevertheless this inner tendency of history to seek definitiveness is a difficult problem. Human freedom is so much conditioned and determined by contingent historical factors that at any one time it can only actualize its own essence fragmentarily. A human being does not possess the freedom of an angel, which is so much in control of itself that it can take decisions about itself once and for all with total validity. Human freedom, in its detailed actualization, always lags behind its essence, and can never adequately be translated into specific physical acts. It is therefore scattered, obscured and ambiguous.Though it has an inner tendency to seek definitiveness, it can never expose this totally in an 'object'. I need not here go into the question whether this inability of human freedom to catch up with itself is part of the essential physical nature of human beings or whether it is a result of the division produced by sin and the concupiscence which surrounds human beings as we know them. The only important thing in this connection is that freedom points forward into a dimension which is not completely within our vision. It means venturing trustfully into a mystery which cannot be elucidated. This is the underlying reason why Christians believe that human freedom definitively 'succeeded' in the crucifixion of Jesus Christ. The love and loyalty of God revealed once for all in the sacrifice of Jesus Christ is the permanent Christian element in history. What is at work in history as a whole only as a tendency and a hope is here actualized. Here a definitive event took place in history, so that the raising of Jesus and the beginning of the new aeon are, as it were, the other side of the cross. Since the cross and raising of Jesus Christ as an eschatological event are the centre of the Christian faith, eschatological definitiveness is an essential feature of Christian faith.[12] Here not every position can be constantly open to revision or replacement, here not everything can be dissolved into a process of permanent reflection and permanent discussion. Without the courage, one could almost say the rashness, to make definitive decisions and statements, the Christian faith would be denying its own nature. But it is here that its strength and power lie. It can promise human beings definitive meaning. A Church which had lost the power to do this would richly deserve to have its preaching ignored, for it would have degenerated into empty mouthings.

9.4 What does infallibility mean?

These reflections have brought me naturally to what is meant by the term 'infallibility'.[13] Until now I have deliberately avoided it because it is notorious for provoking endless misunderstandings. This is a good reason for putting it on ice for a while, to let us keep alive the real principle it embodies. Let me say for a start what it does not involve. Infallibility does not

exclude any kind of failing or flaw. Above all, it does
not mean moral infallibility. It is perfectly possible for
dogmas to be one-sided, superficial, vindictive, stupid
and premature. Nor are propositions infallible which
a priori can in no way be false, propositions which can
contain absolutely no error even when isolated from
their situation and their use. Dogmas are subject to
the historical limitations of all human language, and
are true in detail only in relation to their appropriate
context. This means that they have to be constantly
reinterpreted and translated for new situations. Quot-
ing a dogma proves little; it also has to be interpreted
technically and historically. This process is governed
by the same hermeneutical rules as the interpretation
of any other text. Finally a dogma usually deals with
a truth only from one point of view, and indeed mostly
to circumscribe it negatively and polemically. It therefore does not intend to say, nor can it say, everything
that can and must be said theologically about the particular matter. In general, truth can never be expressed in a single statement, and a dogma therefore
never settles a theological issue once and for all. Infallible dogmas are also not incapable of being im-
proved. Even after they are defined they are affected
by a history of reception, interpretation and integration. They must therefore not be given too much
weight in isolation, but must be interpreted within the
overall testimony of Scripture and tradition.

The first Vatican Council itself does not deny the
historical nature of dogmas. The Council is familiar
with a history of dogma. It does not tie us to the letter
of the formulation, but to the meaning: 'is sensus per-
petuo est retinendus. . . .'[14] We are dealing, not with
infallible propositions, but with an infallible 'cause'.
The 'cause' with which we are dealing is the fact that
with Jesus Christ God's truth came into the world

infallibly: that is, with eschatological definitiveness, and because of God's faithfulness can never more be overcome by falsehood. This central Christological and eschatological statement has to be affirmed historically. What makes this possible, according to the first Vatican Council, is infallible authorities. We are not therefore talking about the infallibility of rigid and lifeless propositions, but about the infallibility of living historical authorities. These authorities can speak historically as a particular situation demands, and can, if necessary, reinterpret their earlier statement historically in a new situation. If there were no infallible witnesses of this sort, it would be impossible for the Gospel to be made present infallibly in history. The Lutheran idea of the self-evidence of the Gospel, of the power and force of the Gospel to keep on establishing its authority and winning a hearing afresh, has an inherent attractiveness, but it has often failed in the history of Protestantism. It also does not take full account of a fundamental principle of the Christian order of salvation, namely that God always acts through human beings. The gospel witness can be made present historically only through the gospel witnesses. Witness and witnesses are mutually dependent.

The principal authority, the one which can claim definitiveness when declaring the Gospel, is the Church as a whole. The Church is the real possessor of infallibility. Only secondarily, because the Church can have an effect only through particular organs, are the college of bishops and its head, the bishop of Rome, a source of infallible statements. In this role, however, the pope and bishops are only spokesmen and representatives of the Church's faith.[15] If they are in danger of falling away from that faith, the other charisms in the Church must rise, call them to order and remind them of their duty. If this action is not successful, and if, in an extreme case, a pope or bishop becomes notoriously heretical and schismatic, there is a large and widespread tradition which maintains that he loses his office. The infallibility of the teaching authority is thus always part of the infallibility of the Church as a whole. If it were possible for the Church as a whole to fall away definitively from faith in Jesus Christ, if it fell away from Christ, it would relapse into the status of the synagogue, God's eschatological and definitive promise in Jesus Christ would have been made null and void, and God would not have shown himself to be God or the Lord of history.

The infallibility of the Church is not strictly a property of the Church, and certainly not an achievement of the Church; what it really involves is the infallibility of God's faithfulness in Jesus Christ. That is the definitive and permanent element in history. Faithfulness is specific. It acts not alongside, but in history. That is why the Church is kept permanently in the truth, not alongside or in spite of its specific doctrinal statements, but in and through them. Faithfulness too, however, is not something rigid and lifeless. We can catch hold of it only in the hope and trust of an answering faithfulness. Having hope in history because of God's faithfulness thus forbids any theology or mood of disaster which believes that there is a general decline in the Church today merely because so much is in ferment. The same hope equally forbids the assumption that everything in the previous history of the Church was a disaster and that the sun of enlightenment is only now beginning to rise on the Church. Both are inadequate faith. Both the over-anxious conservative and the ecclesiastical revolutionary lack real faith. The person who believes is not afraid of history because he knows about the promise which has been set up in history.

This certainty frees us from a timid clinging to old forms and formulas, and frees us for a policy of safety first through boldness (Karl Rahner), based on the conviction that in the present upheaval not prudence, but responsible boldness is the safest thing to gain at least something. If infallibility is understood in this way as an infallibility of hope, it is an evangelical truth in the best sense of the word. True, it does mean that many of the Church's ideas and utterances have to change, and have to be given a happier and more hopeful note.

Notes

1. On what follows, cf. esp. E. Troeltsch, 'Über historische und dogmatische Methode in der Theologie', *Gesammelte Schriften*, vol. II (Tübingen 1913, reprinted Aalen, 1962), pp. 729–53.
2. Cf. G. Krüger, *Freiheit und Weltverantwortung. Aufsätze zur Philosophie der Geschichte* (Freiburg & Munich, 1958), p. 97.
3. On this see A. Darlap, 'Geschichtlichkeit', *LThK* IV² (1960), pp. 780–83; 'Fundamentale Theologie der Heilsgeschichte', J. Feiner and M. Löhrer (ed.), *Mysterium Salutis. Grundriss heilsgeschichtlicher Dogmatik*, vol. I (Einsiedeln & Cologne, 1965), pp. 3–156; G. Bauer, *Geschichtlichkeit. Wege und Irrwege eines Begriffes* (Berlin, 1963); L von Renthe-Finke, *Geschichtlichkeit. Ihr terminologischer und begrifflicher Ursprung bei Hegel, Haym, Dilthey und Yorck*, (Abhandlungen der Akademie der Wissenschaften zu Göttingen (Göttingen, 1964); W. Kasper, *Das Absolute in der Geschichte. Philosophie und Theologie der Geschichte in der Spätphilosophie Schellings* (Mainz, 1965); id., *Glaube und Geschichte.* (Mainz, 1970); P. Hünermann, *Der Durchbruch des geschichtlichen Denkens im 19. Jahrhundert* (Freiburg, 1967); A. Darlap & J. Splett, 'History and Historicity', *Sacramentum Mundi*, vol. III (London, 1969), pp. 31–39.
4. Hegel, *Phenomenology of Spirit*, trans. A. V. Miller, (Oxford, 1977), pp. 11, 27.

174   AN INTRODUCTION TO CHRISTIAN FAITH

5. J. Gründel, *Wandelbares und Unwandelbares in der Moraltheologie* (Düsseldorf, 1967); A. Auer, 'Die Erfahrung der Geschichtlichkeit und die Krise der Moral', *Theologische Quartalschrift* 149 (1969), pp. 4–22.
6. Cf. R. Bultmann, *History and Eschatology* (Edinburgh, 1957). In reaction to the dissolution of history into historicality in existentialist theology, the dimension of real history as extended in time and its theological significance was stressed by Teilhard de Chardin and the theologians influenced by him. The theology of salvation history tends in a similar direction; cf. esp. O. Cullmann, *Christ and Time* (London, 1951, ²1962); *Salvation in History* (London, 1967). On the problems of the concept of salvation history see the short account by H. Ott, *RGG*, vol. III³ (1959), pp. 187–89, s.v. 'Heilsgeschichte'. Subsequently Wolfhart Pannenberg, strongly influenced by Hegel's philosophy of history, attempted to go beyond Barth and Bultmann and define a new basis in universal history, the effect of which can also be seen in the theology of hope (cf. below, n. 9). Cf. W. Pannenberg (ed.) *Revelation as History* (New York & London, 1963); *id.*, *Basic Questions in Theology*, 3 vols, (London, 1970–3); *id.*, *Jesus God and Man* (London, 1968). On the discussion, cf. J. M. Robinson & J. B. Cobb, eds., *Theology as History* (New York & London, 1967).
7. On the theology of non-Christian religions, cf. O. Karrer, *Das Religiöse in der Menschheit und das Christentum* (Frankfurt am Main, ⁴1949); R. Ohm, *Die Liebe zu Gott in den nichtchristlichen Religionen. Die Tatsachen der Religionsgeschichte und die christliche Religion* (Freiburg, ²1957); J. A. Cuttat, *Begegnung der Religionen* (Einsiedeln, 1956); J. Daniélou, *Holy Pagans of the Old Testament* (London, 1957); M. Seckler, *Instinkt und Glaubenswille nach Thomas von Aquin* (Mainz, 1961), pp. 232–58; K. Rahner, 'Christianity and the Non-Christian Religions', *Theological Investigations*, vol. 5, pp. 115–34; H. R. Schlette, *Die Religionen also Thema der Theologie*, Quaestiones Disputatae 22 (Freiburg, 1964); J. Ratzinger, 'Der christliche Glaube und die Weltreligionen', H. Vorgrimler and others (ed.) *Gott in Welt*, vol. II (Freiburg, 1964), pp. 287–305; R. Panikkar, *Religionen und Religionen* (Munich, 1965); H. Fries, 'Das Christentum und die Religionen der Welt', *Wir und die andern* (Stuttgart, 1966); J. Heilsbetz, *Theologische Gründe der nichtchristlichen Religionen*, Quaestiones Disputatae 33 (Freiburg, 1967). For a critical view cf. J. Dörmann, 'Gibt es eine christliche Verheissung für die andern Religionen?', W. Heinen and J. Schreiner (ed.), *Erwartung – Verheissung – Erfüllung*

(Würzburg, 1969), pp. 299–322; M. Seckler, 'Sind Religionen Heilswege?', *StdZ* 95 (1970), pp. 187–94.

8. *Gaudium et Spes*, 3–4; 10–11; 22, 40, 42–3, 44, 62; on the idea of 'the signs of the times'.

9. On the problem of the history of dogma, cf. F. Marin-Sola, *L'Evolution homogène du dogme catholique*, 2 vols (Fribourg, 1924); J. R. Geiselmann, *Lebendiger Glaube aus geheiligter Überlieferung. Der Grundgedanke der Theologie Johann Adam Möhlers und der Katholischen Tübinger Schule* (Mainz, 1942); H. de Lubac, 'Le problème du développement du dogme', *Rech. Sc. Rel.* 35 (1948), pp. 130–60; K. Rahner, 'Considerations on the Development of Dogma', *Theological Investigations*, vol. 4, pp. 3–35; M. Blondel, 'History and Dogma', in *The Letter on Apologetics and History and Dogma*, eds., A. Dru & I. Trethowan (London, 1964); H. Hammans, *Die neuen katholischen Erklärungen der Dogmenentwicklung* (Essen, 1965); W. Kasper, *Dogma unter dem Wort Gottes* (Mainz, 1965); K. Rahner & K. Lehmann, 'Geschichtlichkeit der Vermittlung', *Mysterium Salutis*, vol. I, pp. 727–87; J. Ratzinger, *Das Problem der Dogmengeschichte in der Sicht der Katholischen Theologie* (Cologne, 1966); V. Schulz, *Dogmenentwicklung als Problem der Geschichtlichkeit der Wahrheitserkenntnis* (Rome, 1969); K. Lehmann, 'Die dogmatische Denkform als hermeneutisches Problem', *Ev. Theol.* 30 (1970), pp. 469–87.

10. The importance for Christian faith of an evolutionary view of the world was repeatedly stressed above all by Teilhard de Chardin. On this important fundamental issue cf. also K. Rahner, 'Christology within an Evolutionary View of the World', *Theological Investigations*, vol. 5, pp. 157–92; K. Rahner in P. Overhage, *Um das Erscheinungsbild der ersten Menschen*, Quaestiones Disputatae 7 (Freiburg, 1959), pp. 11–30; K. Rahner, *'Hominisation as a Theological Problem*, Quaestiones Disputatae (London, 1967).

11. Aristotle, *Physics*, 223 a; Augustine, *Confessions* XI, 27, 29.

12. Cf. H. Schlier, *Das Bleibend Katholische. Ein Versuch über ein Prinzip des Katholischen* (Münster, 1970).

13. On what follows cf. H. Küng, *Infallible? An Inquiry* (London & New York, 1971); 'Im Interesse der Sache. Antwort an Karl Rahner', *StdZ* 96 (1971), pp. 43–64, 105–22; K. Rahner (ed.) *Zum Problem der Unfehlbarkeit. Antworten auf die Anfrage von Hans Küng*, Quaestiones Disputatae 54 (Freiburg, 1971); W. Kasper, 'Zur Diskussion um das Problem der Unfehlbarkeit', *StdZ* 96 (1971), pp. 363–76.

14. *DS* 3020 = *NR* 357.

15. *DS* 3074 (= *NR* 388): 'Romanum Pontificem . . . ea infallibilitate pollere qua divinus Redemptor Ecclesiam suam . . . instructam esse voluit' ('The Roman Pontiff . . . enjoys that infallibility with which our divine redeemer wished his Church . . . to be endowed.'). Cf. the statement of Archbishop Gasser, the spokesman of the deputation on faith at the first Vatican Council, that the pope is only infallible 'as the representative of the universal Church' ('universalem ecclesiam repraesentans', Mansi, *Amplissima collectio conciliorum*, vol. 52, 1213 C).

10 The future of faith

10.1 Future of faith – Future of the world

Undoubtedly mankind today is in a critical state of transition. New social, cultural and intellectual developments are apparent throughout a period of profound upheaval and change. In this crisis which affects all areas of our civilization, Christianity too has to undergo criticism. Has Christian faith any future in the society of the future? Can it make any decisive contribution to this future, or will it be condemned to an insignificant marginal existence?

Despair at the future of belief and of the Church lies behind many instances of the present crisis of faith. Many think that religion as a whole and Christianity in particular can have no future in an increasingly technologized and secularized world. Surely, they ask, those functions of the Church which are still carried on with an eye to the future will increasingly be performed by others – by psychotherapists and social workers, for example. . . . In a world ordered by work-plans and feasibility, in a world which in principle is free from the surprising and the astounding, there is in principle no longer any room for the miraculous. Yet the category of the unexpectedly and underivably new is constitutive of Christian faith. Hence there are futurologists who in their prognoses of the future think it is quite appropriate to ignore the religious factor altogether. And there are sociologists, such as Peter Berger, who opine that in the society of the future the Church might continue to exist only as a kind of sect, as a small closed group, sealed and uncommunicative on the periphery of society.[1]

Doubt in the future of Christian faith is one of the most profound challenges to belief. Man is a creature of the future. It is part of his freedom that he should exceed the *status quo*. In facts (that is, in what has become the past and in what is now wholly discernible) there is no room for freedom and creative imagination. The future alone is the realm of open possibilities. It is the area in which freedom takes effect. Therefore mankind is involved in the question of the future. Absolute futurelessness is the very nature of death. Therefore a future without faith would be a dead future. A man directed towards the future would find a faithless future quite unnegotiable. There would be no fascination for anyone in such a prospect. No one would commit himself to such a future. Hence any attempt to establish faith in regard to the special set of problems characteristic of the modern age must take the discernment of the 'future-dimension' of faith as one of its major tasks.

The importance of this endeavour can easily be demonstrated from the experience of the recent history of our Church. The trust and joy in faith which became apparent during the short-lived resurgence of the Church under Pope John XXIII arose largely from this factor. In his famous opening address to the second Vatican Council John XXIII spoke of the future with an optimism which now seems almost naive, and promised the Church a new Pentecost. After this short phase of *aggiornamento*, however, the Church obviously became afraid of its own courage. Now people step back from the risk that freedom and the future obviously entail, and have for the most part placed themselves under the protection of the *status quo* and regressive tendencies. But if the Church becomes the refuge of those who look for security and peace in some world of yesterday, then it should not be astonished when young people turn their back on it, and look for the future to uplifting ideologies and redemptive utopias which promise to fill the vacuum which the Church's pusillanimity has left there.

This is a paradoxical situation. The discovery of the dimension of the future is characteristic of the religion of the Bible. All other religions of the ancient world celebrate no more than the eternal recurrence of sacred origins; they work by a cyclic model. For them there is nothing new under the sun; only that is real which always was and is everlasting.[2] The thought of the Bible breaks through this infernal circle. Here is action and event; here there are real new beginnings which guarantee hope. Here salvation is not at the beginning but a promise for the end of history.

In this way biblical thought cancelled the eternal recurrence of the same. 'Circuitus illi iam explosi sunt', Augustine said triumphantly in the *City of God*.[3] 'The facts are no longer mere phenomena but act and event. Something new is always happening'.[4] For Jesus and the early Church this something new was something that was coming directly. Their imminent expectation allowed them to forget everything else and to forgo everything. It inspired them and empowered them to an enthusiasm which is hardly conceivable for us now. It urged Paul to undertake a mission literally throughout the then known world. Already in the second generation there was a slackening of this eschatological tension.[5] The Church increasingly relegated its eschatological enthusiasm to ranters. It established

itself instead in the world, and became itself an established power and a conservative force. Hence we
should not be surprised if theology too has often forgotten that eschatology represents the horizon of all
Christian faith, and that it must inspire and give its
dynamic thrust to all pronouncements of faith. Eschatology in fact dwindled to a rather inadequate and
poverty-stricken treatise on the 'last things' occupying
an insecure position at the end of our dogmatic asser-
tions. The eschatological dynamism which was increasingly suppressed in official teachings shifted
instead by way of pietistic movements to secular
thought.

The futuristic ideologies and utopias of the modern
age are essentially no more than secular versions of
the biblical hope in the coming of the new man and a
new world. Both the western belief in the future and
in progress, and the Communist hope in a qualitative
leap into a classless society of the future in which all
historical alienations would be overcome, are 'crazy'
Christian ideas which originated in the eschatology of
the Bible.[6] Ultimately, therefore, many people think
that with the category of the future Christianity ex-
ceeded itself. Surely, they object, in the end it made
the future something which extended beyond Christianity. Is the futuristic thrust of the modern age whatever it must now historically become in its own
movement of self-transcendence? Is Christian hope
now something which has to be realized in a secular
and world-historical form?

The answer to be these questions must be a decisive
No. Nothing would be more fateful than to declare
that the dimension of the future is something to be
discovered only once, which is then to be made available thus for all time. The temptation to hold fast to
the apparently secure state of the present moment,

and to the apparently well-proven state of things past, is strong at all times. Again and again we are subject to fear and self-closure before the demands of the future, and to lack of courage to cast off from the shore of what has been and venture into the open seas of the future. That fear is with us today. It is possible even to speak of a fatalism of technological reason, and of a mentality which will trust only that which is clearly lack of faith, fear and scepticism. Any kind of thought that is directed only to what is demonstrable, available and plannable – whatever futurist perspectives it opens up – is only seemingly open to the future. In reality it has to switch off and out any trace of the astonishing, of the wholly new, in order to restrict itself to the facticity of the *status quo*. For any positivistic, technological way of thinking the future can be no more than the extension of the past and of the present. A computerized future would be the end of history. It would be a condemnation merely to extend, improve and confirm existing conditions and circumstances. Anyone who still has any feeling for human freedom and creative imagination can only reject such a possibility with loathing.

The protest of the younger generation has arisen from such a rejection of the vision of an administered, calculated and manipulated world. Ever since the central European youth movements after the first World War this protest has recurred in constantly different forms. One of these forms has however remained the same: it sees the progress and achievements of the modern age as forms of regression and as repression of a truly human human existence. It refuses to remain content with technical and material improvements of existence, if that progress (as seems to be the case with our environmental problems) turns into new threats and thus becomes utterly meaningless. Where history is decided not only by living freedom but by dead facts, not by mankind but by technological and economic laws, the future can only be an inhuman future. Therefore we are in dire need of a critical examination of the future of our society that probes it to the very foundations. The question is obviously whether the critical power of human freedom and the creative force of human imagination are adequate once again to wrest the controls from the established political, economic and technical powers. On the other hand, a violent revolution could lead only to nameless chaos and to an anarchy in which no one could live as a free man or woman.

Are resignation and scepticism then our only course? Here we suddenly see the reality and relevance of the Christian message in a wholly new and unaccustomed way. Christianity with its apparently extremely old-fashioned message of the forgiveness of sins intends nothing other than the possibility of a new beginning and liberation to the future. As the bestowal of a qualitatively new beginning, Christianity is the strength and the courage to stand up against powerful established orders and interests for the sake of the underived New. It is the future of our concerns for the future, and therefore it answers the deepest needs and frustrations of our age. It is the answer to the ultimate intention of the protest movements that are still with us today.

10.2 The new discovery of the eschatological message

It is no accident that the eschatology of the Bible was rediscovered at the very time when the weaknesses and the crisis of the bourgeois world of the new age became clear and new revolutionary ideas arose. This was the achievement of such people as A. Schweitzer, J. Weiss and F. Overbeck. They recognized (as Karl Barth put it later) that a Christianity that was not wholly and completely and thoroughly eschatological had nothing whatsoever to do with Christ.[7] It was not long before the exegetical and historical insights of the years around the turn of the century made their mark in systematic theology. In the great projects of Barth and Bultmann, and of course Rahner and Balthasar, the eschatology of the Bible was still conceived in fundamentally unhistorical categories.[8] Only in the most recent theology has there been a wholly serious confrontation with the structure of hope of Christian faith.[9] There has been a strong influence here from Ernst Bloch's 'philosophy of hope'. But we should not do this theology justice if we merely described it as echoes of the great German philosopher's life-work. Of course the way in which the theology of hope has described the relations between the future within history and the future at the end of history, between the Christian and Marxist forms of hope, has not been wholly successful. But essentially the future has been rediscovered as the essential dimension of Christian faith, and it has been made to afford rich material for dialogue with the contemporary world.

And what is Christianity's vision of the future? Here there are many voices. Somewhat crudely, perhaps, we can distinguish three models[10] which are used to try to determine the eschatological future. Weiss and Schweitzer kept to the direct statements of the New Testament, which treats of the eschatological future largely in the style proper to apocalyptic discourse. Late Jewish apocalyptic represents the events at the end of time pictorially, in the shape of a natural catastrophe. The stars will fall from the heavens and de-

stroy the earth; the earth will succumb to an immense
fire and the new Jerusalem will come down from the
skies in a miraculous way. Most of the New Testament
writings expect the imminent arrival of this new heav-
en and new earth. But the early Christians soon
learned that the Lord delays his coming (Mt. 24:48),
and had to suffer some sharp and ironical questioning
(2 Pet. 3:4). Today the apocalyptic world with its to
some extent repellent ideas and its hardly reconcilable
images has become quite alien. Its dualism of this
world and the world to come permits only a negative
if not a wholly destructive attitude to history. For that
reason revolutionary and Fascist movements have
often made use of apocalyptic notions and images. This
misuse shows something of the danger of the apocalyptic mode.

Therefore people today very often avoid the eschatological and resort instead to the teleological model.
The end of time is seen then not as a catastrophe but
as the completion and fulfilment of history. The eschatological future understood in a teleological sense can
of course be made to accord rather easily with our
present-day evolutionary idea of the world. It can far
too easily be reconciled with the modern belief in progress. Usually Teilhard de Chardin is invoked in this
regard. But not entirely with justice, for Teilhard is
not without certain apocalyptic and prophetic emphases.[11] There are good reasons for that, for what
remains in this harmonious picture of things is the
phenomenon of evil, of unjust suffering; the experience
that history is not merely an upward development but
after epochs of high civilization offers descents into
barbarism and chaos. Therefore teleological thinking
is alien to Scripture. According to the somewhat uniform account offered by the Scriptures, the eschaton
is not only fulfilment but judgment. Here, therefore,

distinction and decision are in question. If this image of judgment is removed in favour of universal eschatological reconciliation, then history loses its decisive seriousness, and ultimately everything is of the same account; then the strict and irreconcilable contrast between good and evil disappears to become a mere polar tension which is finally brought into a grandiose, fugue-like form of harmony and reconciliation. But could we really describe such an ending as the fulfilment of justice and truth? Surely then everything would be essentially equally valid and indifferent? The teleological model is inadequate if we wish to grasp and integrate the legitimate elements of apocalyptic thought.

After the passing of the teleological model based to a great extent on Greek metaphysics and idealistic philosophy, people now think more of the properly biblical understanding of eschatology: the prophetic model.[12] It is older and more fundamental than the apocalyptic pronouncements which occur only since Daniel. Whereas the apocalyptic model recognizes only one subject of history (that is, God), according to the great prophets history occurs as an interplay of divine and human freedom. Naturally divine and human freedom are not on the same level. Ultimately they cannot be reduced one to the other. God's freedom is absolute precedence, transcendence, comprehension. But God's action also means the provocation of human action. It does not suppress but liberates mankind. In this perspective history is taken seriously as history. It is wholly open. God puts the actual coming of his kingdom into human hands. In the decision for belief or unbelief God's rule is also at risk. Only when God's rule is accepted and affirmed in faith has his kingdom really come into history.

If history is understood thus as an interplay of God

and man, then the coming of the *eschata*, the last
things, cannot occur as if according to some kind of
salvific timetable which runs almost deterministically
in accordance with God's eternal decisions. Instead
eternity is decided in history. Since the cross and resurrection of Jesus Christ, eternity has been a matter
of historical becoming. Jesus Christ's obedience to the
cross has established eternity in time through his resurrection. Therefore eternity is not some prepared
space which has existed from time immemorial, and
into which at the end of time all the redeemed will
enter in a joyful procession accompanied by angels
singing hosannah. The procession into eternity begins
now. In this perspective history is entirely subject to
God's promise and yet is wholly entrusted to human
responsibility. It is *kairos*, the hour of grace and the
hour of judgment, which decides about eternity.

If we take this prophetic model seriously, then the
much-invoked antitheses of eschatology within history
and eschatology at the end of history disappear. Despite all necessary distinctions, both belong together
in a biblically-oriented eschatology. 'Future' comes
from the Latin *futurum*, from *fuo*, I shall be, and cor-
responds to the Greek φύω and its substantive φύσις.
Physis is the productive, the eternally generative and
bearing womb of all things, process as the actualization of primary potentiality. But future also stands for
adventus and παρουσίχ. Here future means arrival and
presence, the underivable that-which-is-to-come, the
self-bestowing. Future as mere *futurum* is extrapolat-
ed, but as *adventus* is anticipated. The characteristic
feature of prophetic thought, however, is that it allows
no irreconcilable antithesis between the two. God's
future liberates mankind for their own future; it intends in judgment the salvation of the world. This is
evident in regard to modern ideologies and utopias of

the future. Whereas Christianity stands for future
(and therefore meaningful fulfilment) here and now,
the ideologies transfer any expectation of salvation to
a non-temporal future. Hence they are extremely alien
to the world; they demand that any present generation
should sacrifice itself for the sake of a utopian future.
They do not cancel but increase the alienations from
which people suffer. It is not Christianity but the modern futuristic ideologies which (when we examine
them closely) rely not on a beyond (in which at least
everyone would participate), but on a future which
those who now labour and are heavy-laden will neither
see nor experience.

The finality which, according to Christian belief,
occurs in history is ultimately nothing other than God
himself. As the God of hope (Rom. 15:13), he is also
the future of mankind and of history. At that point
where the psalmist expresses his most profound and
ultimate hope, he is no longer concerned with this or
that, with possessions or well-being, with honour or
power; it is simply a matter of: 'Whom have I in heaven
but thee? And there is none upon earth that I desire
beside thee' (Ps. 72/3:25). Here everything cosmologi-
cal is demythologized in eschatological hope and interpreted theologically – in the original sense of the
word.[13] God as the ultimate victor is heaven; God as
the ultimate loser is hell; God as the purifying fire of
love is what we call the fires of hell. Just as we define
the *eschata* through God, so God is defined through
the *eschata*. The *eschaton* means not only something
for man and for history, but something for God. Only
at the end, when everything has returned to him, will
he be all in all (1 Cor. 15:28).

This is a daring notion in the light of Greek metaphysics and its concept of God's unchangeability. It
means that God's being is in a process of unfolding

(Ernst Jüngel). God's divine being is apparent in that he enters into history without being dissolved into it. He is not a developing God who only realizes himself and achieves his own fulness in history and through it. But in his love that is self-bestowal he is that which is supremely free. He shows forth his quality as the Lord in and through history.[14] Hence the eschatological perspective qualifies all pronouncements of faith. It is the horizon in which we have to see theology as anthropology, the study of God as the study of man. Therefore we can summarily describe Christianity as the religion of the absolute future.[15] This definition is threefold:

1. Christianity is a religion of the future. It does not understand reality as an eternal, fixed order, but as history which is directed to a greater future. It teaches us to go beyond all that is given, the *status quo*, to its greater possibilities. It is not the religion of the sated and self-satisfied but the religion of those who hunger and thirst after justice. Faith in the kingdom of God brings us not only peace but lack of peace. It is not an opium that puts us to sleep but a moving ferment.

2. Christianity is the religion of the absolute future. It cannot itself make projects and prognoses for the future which are directly within history. Therefore it is not directly competitive with such projections of the future within history. It enters into deadly conflict with them when they claim to be absolute and become totalitarian in regard to human freedom. Hence Christianity as the religion of the absolute future is the crisis of human *hubris*. But it is also courage to strive for a better historical future. If it is true that love always remains (1 Cor. 13:8), then it is also true that the works of love always remain, and that every-thing done out of love is forever established in the **condition of reality.**

3. As the religion of the absolute future, Christianity itself will always have a future. It not only stands for an irreplaceable future; it is itself grounded in the future that it proclaims. It is established in the eschatological nature of the Christ-event that there will always be a Church. That does not enable us to make any concrete deductions about the actual appearance of the Church's future, and how we are to shape it in actuality. Christian faith contains neither the promise that countries and continents that once were Christian will always remain so, nor the promise that the greater part of mankind will always be Christian. In this regard everything is literally open, and there is hardly cause for an easy optimism on the part of anyone who sees things as they really are. The hope that is based on the cross can only be a crucified hope. It excludes all forms of the Church triumphant. Moreover, poverty and persecution are characteristics of the true Church of Christ. The future of the Church can only be this: though perplexed it will not be lacking in courage; though oppressed it will not be overwhelmed (cf. 2 Cor. 4:7–9).

10.3 The future form of faith

Although eschatology cannot be a kind of prediction, we are not forbidden to consider the actual historical future of faith. The problems are profoundly urgent, and above all we must ask what light the rediscovery of the eschatological perspective of faith on the present world-situation can shed on the future form of faith. I shall now try to outline this kind of theological 'futurology' in three aspects.

The rediscovery of the eschatological perspective of Christian faith means primarily a rediscovery of the decisive viewpoint from which we can see what is specifically Christian. For Overbeck the loss of an eschatological perspective was the loss of the very Christianity of Christendom. Of course there is no question of a total loss. However, if nowadays we see the eschatological nature of faith more clearly, then it must be a characteristic of the faith of the future that it should be more conscious, decisive and essential. External factors will also contribute to that in future. Faith – in so far as we can affirm this at present – will become less and less a universally recognized major phenomenon and an obvious social fact. More important, however, than this more external viewpoint is the fact that a more exact recognition of the eschatological nature of Christianity will also bring about a moce conscious demarcation from within. The acknowledgment that the salvation of the world occurred once and for all in Jesus Christ is the prime scandal of Christian faith. This scandalous fact of Christian hope forbids all vagueness. It is the ground of what is decisively and distinctively Christian.

The results for the practice of faith in this 'eschatological thorn' cannot easily be overestimated. Early on, de-eschatologization led to a kind of 'bourgeoisification' of Christianity, and to its establishment in the world. Since Constantine, Christianity has often identified itself with the *status quo* and bowed to the rulers of the time. But it is just as characteristic of Christianity that almost all its martyrs offered their testimony in resistance to the political power. When Christianity was at the height of its witness to faith, it was critical. Today, at least in the West, danger no longer threatens from state power, but from other social forces – especially from public and published opinion. All the socio-critical emotion which is now evident in theology cannot conceal the fact that the urgently-needed opening up of the Church to the world is sometimes in danger of succumbing to public opinion. Some critics should not be more uncritical, but more critical instead of uncritically following everything that sounds critical. If openness to the world is uncritical and naive, and all distinctions are removed, then neither the Church nor the world is well served. Only if it is critical can the thrust of the Gospel become a power which breaks through the barrier of apparent axioms and in that way makes room for more freedom and more humanity.

The faith that makes clear what is really Christian has to be a critical faith. If you find the word 'critical' too fashionable, then you can use 'penitential' or 'contrite' instead. That is what I mean by 'critical' here. Repentance is the most radical form of criticism. It demands a conversion that is quite radical, that reaches down to the very roots. It is grounded in the eschatological conversion of all things. Moreover, criticism understood thus can and must exist inside the Church in the future. The stress on the eschatological nature of faith also means a change in our understanding of the ecclesial nature of faith. If the eschatological difference between the Church and the kingdom of God, between Christ and the Church, is taken seriously, then the Church can no longer see itself directly as a representation of God, or as an extension of Christ (*Christus prolongatus*). By advancing this claim in the past it has often immunized itself to all criticism, and shuffled off criticism as evidence of that which is alien to the Church, or even of unbelief. If, however, it is acknowledged that in the Gospel the Church possesses a norm which is precedent and superior to it, then it is possible to have a theologically-justified form of criticism in the Church. Since this criticism stems from the very essence of the Gospel and expresses its critical eschatological character (*crisis*), it is more radical than all external criticism. It takes the Church so to speak as its own word, and tries to change it from within. Hence it is not a dominant and distant critique from above, but passionately committed criticism. It includes the critic. It is passionate and suffering criticism. Its only goal must be to elicit what is distinctively and decisively Christian and to make it a form of provocation in the Church itself.

The second element of a future form of faith which will once again exist consciously from an eschatological perspective, is its universality and catholicity. The eschatological promise includes the promise of universal peace and of the universal reconciliation of all mankind. The Old Testament awaits at the end of time the procession of the nations to Jerusalem (Is. 2:2–5; 60; Mich. 4:1–3). The New Testament sees the universal missionary task as the initial realization of this eschatological hope. Today, for various reasons that I cannot describe in detail here, mission work is in a severe state of crisis. Nowadays the vision of a united mankind would seem to be working out in a different way. A single world-civilization is increasingly emerging on the basis of science and technology and a new humanism. This secular ecumenism has fundamentally altered the situation of Christian faith and has put Christianity directly alongside all nations and religions and the great human problems of the present day. This situation demands a Christianity on a world-scale. It asks for a Christianity which will discard its predominantly European form and realize its catholicity and universality in a new way. But this situation also puts on Christianity the burden of an enormous universal responsibility. Today it is becoming ever clearer that western civilization does not of itself possess the power to create one mankind and to afford human fulfilment. As an historical religion Christianity alone should be in a position to offer meaning and security in a world that has developed historically, and to provide the inward and outward integration of mankind. Only the salvific ideology of Marxism really offers any serious counterpart to Christianity in this regard. Hence an eschatologico-apocalyptical outlook is something contemporary Christianity has to adopt. Christianity has to prove itself in a universal perspective, and has to show how Christian faith is a means to truly humane solutions to contemporary human problems.

In this new epoch of a universal human civilization, the fundamental form of faith will be the combined love of God and of one's neighbour.[16] That is at the centre of Jesus' eschatological message. It forms part of the best Christian tradition throughout the centuries. Today it requires from us a fraternal faith that shows its solidarity with human needs. Ultimately, the decisive new form of understanding of existence is expressed by Christianity in this united faith and love. The highest thing is not substance which exists in and for itself, but love which exists for others. In the future, that should result in a new form of holiness and spirituality. It should unite the greatest possible openness with the greatest possible decisiveness of faith. It is certainly the greatest lack of the contemporary Church that it does not yet possess this charisma, this form of holiness. Hence it is torn between an openness which runs insubstantially into a universal humanism, and a self-engaged decisiveness which continues uncommunicatively alongside the problems of mankind today, and which could ultimately force the Church into the danger of a sectarian mentality.

It is possible to summarize the third element of the faith of the future in the statement: Christian faith will be simpler. In the future Christianity will almost certainly lose even more of the social and cultural gloss of past centuries. It will have to throw off some hard-won ideas, forms of piety and religious organizations. It will be outwardly poorer and quantitatively it will surely be only a minority within the whole population of the world. This law of increasing simplicity also applies to faith itself. It would certainly be naive to assert that in the future the Church could rid itself of its dogmas either in part or altogether. But these dogmas are answers to questions which are no longer directly our own questions. They are increasingly directly accessible only to historians, and the historical consciousness is continually diminishing. If Christian faith is not to become empty and insubstantial, and if it is not merely to accord with whatever is most fashionable, then it must grow more in profoundity than in width, and live more consciously from its all-embracing centre. In this sense, too, Christian faith will become simpler in the future.

This centre which comprises everything is nothing more than the basic idea behind everything I have said up to now, and which I shall now repeat in summary form: The message of God's divine existence is that which makes possible man's human existence. It is the secret longing of history; the centre of Jesus' message of the kingdom of God; and the essential idea of the Church's salvific mission. Jesus Christ united both things in his own person. Precisely in his fully human obedience he is a true man and true God. Therefore he is the rule of God in person. With him it has finally begun. Through him hope has ultimately become possible for us. He is the lasting measure of all Christian and church activity. Therefore we can say: Whoever believes that in Jesus Christ hope has been revealed for us and for all mankind, and whoever ventures on that basis to become in real terms a figure of hope for others, is a Christian. He holds in a fundamental sense the whole Christian faith, even though he does not consciously accept all the deductions which in the course of almost two thousand years the Church has made from this message. If we make the message of God's rule and kingdom the centre of theology, then we return to approaches which played a rôle mainly for certain theologians of the Enlightenment and, more profoundly, for certain representatives of the Catholic Tübingen School in the nineteenth century.[17] The theology of the schools did not follow these approaches. It was frightened off by the misuse which pietistic movements made of them. But, together with ranting and pietism, it also dispensed largely with the universal perspective of the message of the kingdom of God. Now we must free ourselves of such restrictions. Only if we emphasize not merely the unambiguous nature of faith but its universality, and if we preserve its unambiguousness in its universality, can Christian faith shine as a light on a candlestick. Only then can it have any real future in a new historical age.

Notes

    1. Peter Berger, *The Sacred Canopy* (New York, 1967); *Id.*, *Facing up to Modernity* (New York, 1977; Harmondsworth, 1979); *id.*, P. Berger & H. Kellner, *The Homeless Mind* (New York, 1973). On the following, see also W.-D. Marsch, *Zukunft* (Stuttgart & Berlin, 1969).
    2. See Mircea Eliade, *The Myth of the Eternal Return* (London, 1954).
    3. Augustine, *De Civitate Dei*, 1. 12, c.20, n. 3: *PL* 41, 371.
    4. Henri de Lubac, *Catholicism* (London & New York, 1950); *id.*, *The Splendour of the Church* (London & New York, 1955).

5. The problem of de-eschatologization was posed in the wake of the radical-eschatological conception put forward by J. Weiss and A. Schweitzer. See on this point W. G. Kümmel's survey in *The New Testament: The History of the Investigation of its Problems* (London, 1973), esp. pp. 276–81; *id.*, *Heilsgeschehen und Geschichte* (Marburg, 1965). In regard to systematics, this problem is emphasized not only by F. Buri but in the monumental (though also monomanic) work of M. Werner, *Die Entstehung des christlichen Dogmas* (Berne & Tübingen, ²1955). On the history of theology and the history of the Church in this respect, see B. Kötting, 'Von der Naherwartung der frühen Kirche zur christlichen Hoffnung auf die Endzeit', in: *Erwartung-Verheissung-Erfüllung*, eds, W. Heinen & J. Schreiner (Würzburg, 1969), pp. 184–205; P. Müller-Goldkuhle, in *Concilium* 5 (1969).

6. Cf. Karl Löwith, *Weltgeschichte und Heilgeschehen* (Stuttgart, ⁴1961).

7. Cf. Karl Barth, *The Epistle to the Romans* (London, 1933).

8. An account of contemporary discussions of eschatology is to be found in: Hans Urs von Balthasar, 'Eschatologie', in: *Fragen der Theologie heute*, eds, J. Feiner *et al.* (Einsiedeln & Cologne, 1957), pp. 403–21; G. Greshake, *Auferstehung der Toten* (Essen, 1969).

9. See Jürgen Moltmann, *Theology of Hope* (London, 1967); Gustavo Gutierrez, *A Theology of Liberation* (New York, 1971; London, 1974); Ernst Bloch, *Man on his Own* (New York, 1970); *id.*, *Philosophy of the Future* (New York, 1971); J.-B. Metz, *Theology of the World* (London, 1969); *id.*, *Faith in History and in Society* (London & New York, 1980). We might criticize the theology of the future for its inadequate stress on the relation of eschatology to protology (creation and redemption), and for the consequent danger of conversion to an unqualified revolutionary dynamism of the future.

10. Cf. Harvey Cox on evolution and Christian promise in *Concilium* 3 (1967).

11. See S. Daecke, *Teilhard de Chardin und die evangelische Theologie* (Göttingen, 1967).

12. Cf. G. Greshake, *Auferstehung der Toten*, *op. cit.*

13. See J. Moltmann, 'Antwort auf die Kritik der Theologie der Hoffnung', in: *Diskussion über die 'Theologie der Hoffnung'*, ed. W.-D. Marsch (Munich, 1967), pp. 210ff.

14. On the hermeneutics of eschatological statements, see Hans Urs von Balthasar, *Eschatologie*, *op. cit.*; Karl Rahner in

Theological Investigations Vol. IV (London, 1964); E. Schillebeeckx
in *Concilium* 5 (1969).
    15. Cf. E. Jüngel, *Gottes Sein ist im Werden* (Tübingen, 1965);
Hans Küng, *Menschwerdung Gottes* (Freiburg, 1970), pp. 611–
70; Leslie Dewart, *The Future of Belief* (London & New York,
1967).
    16. On the following see Karl Rahner on the Marxist utopia
and the Christian future of mankind in *Theological Investigations*
Vol. VI (London 1967).
    17. See Karl Rahner on the unity of the love of neighbour and
the love of God, in *ibid.*
    18. W. Nigg, *Das ewige Reich* (Erlenbach & Zürich, 1944); K.
Löwith, *Weltgeschichte und Heilgeschehen, op. cit.;* E. Staehlin,
Die Verkündigung des Reiches Gottes in der Kirche Jesus Christi,
6 vols. (Basle, 1951–63); J. R. Geiselmann, *Die Katholische
Tübinger Schule* (Freiburg, 1964), pp. 191–279; A. Hertz *et al.,*
Gottesreich und Menschenreich (Regensburg, 1971).

Abbreviations

DS H. Denzinger & A. Schönmetzer, *Enchiridion Symbolorum, Definitionum et Declarationum de rebus fidei et morum* (Freiburg i. Br., [33]1965).

EKL *Evangelisches Kirchenlexikon. Kirchlich-theologisches Handwörterbuch*, eds., H. Brunotte & O. Weber, 4 vols. (Göttingen, 1955–61).

FRLANT *Forschungen zur Religion und Literatur des Alten- und Neuen Testaments* (Göttingen, 1930ff).

HthG *Handbuch theologischer Grundbegriffe*, ed., H. Fries, 2 vols. (Munich, 1962–3).

LTK *Lexikon für Theologie und Kirche*, eds., J. Höfer & Karl Rahner (Freiburg i. Br., [2]1957ff).

NR J. Neuner & H. Roos, *Der Glaube der Kirche in den Urkunden der Lehrverkündigung*, ed., K. Rahner (Regensburg, [7]1965).

RAC *Reallexikon für Antike und Christentum*, ed., T. Klauser (Stuttgart, 1941ff).

RGG *Die Religion in Geschichte und Gegenwart, Handwörterbuch für Theologie und Religionswissenschaft*, ed., K. Galling (Tübingen, [3]1956ff).

StdZ *Stimmen der Zeit* (before 1914: *Stimmen aus Maria-Laach*) (Freiburg i. Br., 1871ff).

TWNT *Theologisches Wörterbuch zum Neuen Testament*, ed., G. Kittel, cont., G. Friedrich (Stuttgart, 1933ff).

WW *Gesammelte Werke* (collected works).

ZTK   *Zeitschrift für Theologie und Kirche*
           (Tübingen, 1891ff).

Index of names

A

Adam, Karl 112
Adorno, Friedrich 8, 17, 18, 66
Albert, H. 65
Alfaro, J. 71, 90, 133
Aner, K. 17
Anz, W. 17
Aquinas, St Thomas 66, 72, 110, 113, 114, 129, 134, 140, 153
Aristotle 167, 175
Arnold, F. X. 132, 153
Aubert, R. 90
Auer, A. 174
Augustine, St 2, 167, 175, 179, 195

B

Barth, Karl 12, 17, 20, 54, 174, 183, 196
Bartley, W. 65
Bauer, G. 173
Berger, P. L. 153, 178, 195
Bernet, W. 91
Biser, E. 134
Bishop, J. 16
Bleistein, R. 113
Bloch, Ernst 69, 183, 196
Blondel, Maurice 61, 90, 175
Blumenberg, H. 17
Bonaventure 133
Bonhoeffer, Dietrich 36, 137, 153
Bornkamm, Günter 43, 53
Bouillard, H. 90, 118, 132
Brecht, Bertolt 84
Brentano, Franz 9, 154
Brunner, P. 111

Buber, Martin 80, 91, 161
Bultmann, Rudolf 40, 41, 42, 43, 48, 53, 56,
   70, 71, 90, 112, 133, 153, 174, 183
Buri, F. 196

C

Cassirer, Ernst 16
Cirne-Lima, C. 90
Claudel, Paul 9
Cobb, J. B. 174
Congar, Yves 153
Constantine 190
Conzelmann, H. 52, 53, 54, 112, 133, 134, 153
Cortes 9
Cox, Harvey 17, 133, 134, 196
Cragg, G. R. 17
Cullmann, Oskar 53, 112, 174
Cuttat, J. A. 174

D

Daecke, S. 196
Daniélou, Jean 174
Darlap, Adolf 173
de Bonald, Louis 9
de Ghellink, J. 112
Delaye, E. 132
Delling, G. 70
de Lubac, Henri 112, 118, 132, 175, 195
de Maistre, Joseph 9
Descartes, René 11, 75
Dewart, Leslie 197
Dibelius, Martin 40
Dombois, H. 152, 153

Hünermann, P.   173
Hus, John   138

J

Jeremias, J.   91
John XXIII, Pope   178
Jüngel, E.   36, 187–8, 197

K

Kahl, J.   115, 132
Kant, Immanuel   5, 17, 18, 26, 36
Karrer, O.   174
Käsemann, Ernst   41, 42, 46, 53, 126, 134, 153
Kasper, Walter   18, 71, 113, 173, 175
Kattenbusch, F.   112
Kegel, G.   70
Kellner, H.   195
Kelly, J. N. D.   112
Kessler, H.   134
Kierkegaard, Søren   12, 18
Kittel, G.   71, 91
Kolping, A.   53
Kötting, B.   196
Kramer, W.   112
Kreck, W.   134
Kremer, J.   70
Krüger, G.   173
Kuhn, J. E.   10
Kümmel, W. G.   52, 196
Küng, Hans   36, 71, 113, 153, 175
Kunz, E.   72

L

Lauth, R. 36
Lehmann, K. 70, 111, 112, 113, 175
Leibniz, Gottfried Wilhelm 10
Lengsfeld, P. 16
Lessing, G. E. 11, 18, 62, 71
Leuba, J. L. 153
Lietzmann, H. 112
Löhrer, M. 173
Lohse, E. 134
Lohse, J. M. 132
Loisy, A. 136, 152
Löwith, Karl 17, 196
Lübbe, H. 17
Luckmann, Thomas 153
Ludochowski, H. 70

M

Machovec, M. 36
Maier, H. 133
Malmberg, F. 71
Marchel, W. 91
Marcion 118
Marin-Sola, F. 175
Maritain, Jacques 9
Marsh, W. D. 152, 195
Marx, Karl 12, 18, 26, 157, 183, 193
Marxsen, Willi 54, 56, 70, 71
Matthes, J. 152
Maurer, W. 17
Metz, Johann Baptist 17, 53, 72, 91, 133, 196
Möhler, J. A. 10, 142, 152, 154, 163
Moltmann, Jürgen 36, 91, 133, 196
Mourous, J. 90
Mühlen, Heribert 113

Müller, W. 17
Müller-Goldkuhle, P. 196
Muschalek, G. 72, 90
Mussner, Franz 53, 54, 70

N

Nantin, P. 113
Nestle, D. 134
Neufeld, V. H. 112
Meumann, J. 113
Newman, John Henry 9, 142, 153
Nietzsche, Friedrich 1, 8, 17, 18, 167
Nigg, Walter 197

O

Ohm, R. 174
Olmüller, W. 17, 91, 133
Ott, H. 174
Overbeck, F. 183, 190

P

Palmer, K. 71
Panikkar, Raymond 174
Pannenberg, Wolfhart 54, 132, 174
Pascal, Blaise 15, 18, 20, 35, 159
Paul, St 59, 80, 81, 97, 126, 140, 151, 179
Pesch, O. H. 91, 133
Pesch, R. 53
Peukert, H. 133
Picht, G. 18
Pieper, Josef 90
Pius XI, Pope 100
Popper, Karl 65
Pottmeyer, J. H. 71

Q

Quell, G. 71

R

Rahner, Karl 2, 16, 36, 91, 113, 132, 133, 163, 173, 174, 175, 183, 196, 197
Ratschow, C. H. 112
Ratzinger, J. 54, 111, 112, 113, 133, 174, 175
Reimarus, Hermann Samuel 39
Renan, Ernest 39
Rendtorff, T. 133, 152
Rengstorf, K. H. 70
Richardson, A. 17
Richter, W. 111
Ricken, F. 54
Robinson, John 36, 84–5, 91
Robinson, J. M. 53, 174
Rohrmoser, G. 17
Rondet, H. 132
Rothe, R. 152
Rousselot, Pierre 65, 72

S

Sallust 159
Schäfer, K. 54
Schafer, R. 91, 112
Scheeben, J. M. 117
Scheffczyk, L. 132
Schelling, F. W. 18
Schelsky, H. 152, 153
Schillebeeckx, E. 36, 91, 133, 197
Schlatter, A. 71, 90
Schleiermacher, F. 39
Schletter, H. R. 174
Schlier, H. 54, 70, 112, 113, 132, 133, 175

Schmaus, M. 112
Schmid, J. 53
Schnackenburg, Rudolf 53, 90
Schrage, W. 134
Schreiner, J. 111, 174
Schrenk, G. 91
Schulz, V. 175
Schürmann, Heinrich 53, 133
Schweitzer, Albrecht 38–9, 52, 183, 196
Schweizer, E. 112
Seckler, M. 90, 133, 174, 175
Seeberg, A. 112
Seidensticker, P. 70
Semler, Solomon 158
Semmelroth, O. 132
Simon, Richard 158
Slenczka, R. 52
Sohm, R. 153
Sölle, Dorothee 74, 84, 90, 91
Spaemann, R. 17
Splett, J. 173
Staehlin, E. 197
Staudenmaier, F. A. 10
Stock, A. 113
Strauss, D. F. 39, 158
Stromberg, R. N. 17
Sudbrack, J. 91

T

Teilhard de Chardin, Pierre 174, 175, 184
Thum, B. 53
Tillich, P. 132, 167
Tödt, H. E. 133
Trethowan, Illtyd 175
Troeltsch, Ernst 155, 156, 173
Trütsch, J. 90

V

W

Z